Ask Suze®

. . . About Insurance

ALSO BY SUZE ORMAN

You've Earned It, Don't Lose It

Suze Orman's Financial Guidebook

The 9 Steps to Financial Freedom

The Courage to Be Rich

The Road to Wealth

The Laws of Money, The Lessons of Life

The Money Book for the Young, Fabulous & Broke

Women & Money

Riverhead Books
a member of
Penguin Group (USA) Inc.
New York
2007

Ask Suze®

...About Insurance

SUZE ORMAN

This publication is designed to provide accurate and authoritative information in regard to the subject matter covered. It is published with the understanding that the publisher and author are not engaged in rendering legal, accounting, or other professional services. If legal advice or other professional advice, including financial, is required, the services of a competent professional person should be sought.

While the author has made every effort to provide accurate telephone numbers and Internet addresses at the time of publication, neither the publisher nor the author assumes any responsibility for errors, or for changes that occur after publication.

Ask Suze® is a federally registered mark owned by Suze Orman.

People First, Then Money, Then Things™ is a trademark owned by Suze Orman.

Certified Financial Planner® is a federally registered mark owned by the Certified Financial Planner Board of Standards, Inc.

The term Realtor® is a collective membership mark owned by the National Association of Realtors® and refers to a real estate agent who is a member thereof.

RIVERHEAD BOOKS
a member of
Penguin Group (USA) Inc.
375 Hudson Street
New York, NY 10014

Published simultaneously in Canada

ISBN 978-1-59448-964-8

Printed in the United States of America
1 3 5 7 9 10 8 6 4 2

Book design by Deborah Kerner and Claire Vaccaro

Ask Suze®

. . . about Insurance

Preparing for the Unexpected

Having the right kind of insurance at the right stage of life is an essential part of any good financial plan. Yet, over the years, I've discovered that many people find buying insurance a daunting task. With hundreds of different policy options available for each type of insurance—including health, home, car, and life—figuring out the kind of policy you should have and the amount of coverage you need can be time-consuming and baffling. Sometimes even choosing the *type* of insurance you need may be difficult. And once you've decided on the appropriate kind and amount of insurance, it may not be what the insurance agent wants to sell you, which only adds to the confusion.

Take, for example, the "whole life" life insurance policy your agent may have sold you many years ago. I'll bet you're still hanging on to it. "Well, why not?" you might ask. We all need insurance coverage as we get older, don't we? Yes, we do. But for the majority of you, the kind of insurance you need as you age is term, not whole, life. You probably *do* need long-term care insurance, which many of us know very little about.

Evaluating basic insurance needs at different times in your life is financial self-protection at its most fundamental and involves a primary lesson of planning for financial freedom: respecting your money and being careful about the choices you make with it. You certainly can't count on salespeople to be careful for you.

As you read this chapter, you may come to realize that you have bought a policy that you do not need. Not to worry: This is a problem that can be fixed, and I will show you how to fix it. Before you act, however, I implore you to read the entire chapter and to always secure new insurance coverage before you drop old policies. A new policy won't help you if something happens to you a week before it becomes effective.

Let's begin by addressing the most basic questions about insurance: what type of insurance you need, what kind of policy will work best, and what amount of coverage you should have.

INSURANCE BASICS

What is insurance, anyway?

All insurance policies are like a bet between you and the insurance company. The company agrees to reimburse you for the cost of your losses—for example, the loss of your health, or the loss of your house in a fire, or the premature loss of your life. The insurance provider is betting, however, that over the long run, you will be safe and healthy and pay more in premiums and deductibles than the company will pay you in benefits. Usually the company is right. Your bet—a crucial one—is that maybe it won't be. The premiums you pay and the deductibles that you agree to buy you the peace of mind that comes with knowing that your assets will be protected, whatever happens.

Are there special guidelines to follow when buying all types of insurance?

Yes. Whenever you buy insurance of any kind, make sure you've done the following:

- *Compare policies.* Always shop around to be sure that you're getting the best policy for your money. Remember, however, that the cheapest policy will not always be the best one for you. Don't compare only costs; compare resources and services, too.
- *Ask yourself the following questions:*

  Have you read every word of the insurance policy that you are buying?

  Do you understand the definitions the insurance company uses?

  What will your policy specifically cover?

  What will your policy specifically not cover?

  What will it take to qualify for your benefits?

- *Review your policies each year* and make sure that they are still responsive to your needs. Have you made major improvements to your house? Did your youngest child finish college? Did your spouse become eligible for Social Security? Have you and your spouse divorced? These kinds of life changes may mean that your insurance coverage should change, too.

What is a premium?

A premium is the price you pay for your insurance coverage, whether or not the benefits are paid. Your premiums will vary depending on, among other things, how much protection you want to buy, how long your policy will last, the size of your deductible, your age, your health, and how often you make payments.

What is a deductible?

If you need to make a claim on your insurance policy, the deductible is the amount of money you will have to pay out of pocket before the insurance company will begin to pay any benefits. Depending on your policy, your deductible can be either a fixed dollar amount or a percentage of the total cost of your claim. In other words, you could be responsible for paying the first $500 of a claim, or you could be responsible for 10 percent of the total amount of a claim. Deductibles often have an annual limit beyond which you are not required to pay anything, even if you have additional claims.

What is coinsurance?

Coinsurance is the fixed percentage of the covered fees that you are required to pay after your deductible has been subtracted from the amount of money owed on a particular claim. Coinsurance requirements are found, mostly, in health insurance policies. So if you have a policy that requires you to pay a $300 deductible and 20 percent coinsurance, and you have medical bills of, say, $1,300, you would be responsible for $300 (your deductible) plus 20 percent of the remaining $1,000, or $200 (coinsurance). In this example, the claim would cost you a total of $500, while the insurance would pay $800.

Insurance premiums are so expensive. Is there any way to reduce them?

It always pays to compare policies from different insurance companies. When you do, you'll find that increasing your deductible generally lowers your regular premiums. But before leaping to that option, be sure that you will be able to afford the higher deductible. There's no point in lowering a high premium by agreeing to pay a $5,000 deductible if, in the event that you need to pay it, you won't have the money! This is a good example of the principle that money attracts money: If you can save enough in an emergency fund to cover a higher deductible, you can afford to take this risk and save money on your premiums. By the same token, if you've got the money to pay your premium once a year, rather than spreading it out, you may find savings of about 8 percent in overall costs. Another possible way to save money is by purchasing multiple insurance policies from the same company. (But be sure to compare the costs of other companies' policies before you commit to a single insurer.)

What does it mean if a policy is guaranteed renewable, and why is this important?

It is extremely important, because it means that the insurance company guarantees that it will renew your policy—usually a health or life policy—every year, regardless of what health problems you may develop over time. In other words, as long as you told the truth on your application—about, for example, any so-called preexisting health conditions—and continue to pay your premiums, your coverage cannot be cut off.

So guaranteed renewable policies are a must, right?

Definitely. You don't want your coverage canceled if you've gone to the trouble of finding a good plan.

How do I buy insurance?

Most people use insurance agents, who make their livings by earning commissions on the policies they sell you. A growing number of financial planners, accountants, and attorneys are also selling insurance these days. You can often buy insurance directly from the insurance company, but you will most likely still pay a commission. You can also buy insurance over the Internet, through your place of work, through membership organizations, or through nonprofit groups to which you belong. How to buy insurance and whom to buy it from will never be a problem; there's no end to the number of people who will try to sell you insurance. The key is to buy the best insurance for your needs at the most cost-effective price.

My neighbor says I need to make sure that my insurance agent is independent. Is that true?

Absolutely! Independent agents, who are sometimes called brokers, can sell you insurance from any of many different insurance companies and are supposed to get you the best possible deal. The opposite of an independent agent is a "captive" agent—a person employed by a particular insurance company, who is authorized to sell you only the policies of that company. In most circumstances, you do not want to deal with a captive agent.

So why do people use captive agents?

Because they don't know better. People just walk into an insurance company, or are solicited by one, and assume that because the company is reputable they will get a good deal. You want an independent agent who's free to offer you every policy issued by every insurer. The way to a good deal is comparison shopping. A captive agent can't help you there.

I read a magazine article about low-load insurance companies. Do they offer good deals?

These are companies that sell their policies directly, not

through an agent. This is supposed to save them money, which they then can pass on to you. But unless you're willing to do the research to figure out exactly which insurance policies you want, you will be better off with an independent agent, who knows more than you do.

What do the letters CLU and CPCU mean on my insurance agent's card?

CLU stands for Chartered Life Underwriter. CPCU stands for Chartered Property and Casualty Underwriter. Both are designations that must be earned through a combination of accredited courses, rigorous exams, and experience in the field.

Even if your agent or broker hasn't earned a CLU or CPCU designation, they must be licensed by the state they work in. If you want to make sure your agent is licensed, you can call your state's insurance department. At the same time, you can find out whether or not there have been complaints filed against the insurance company or agent you are using or considering using.

How can I tell if an insurance company is reliable and financially viable?

Four separate rating services rate insurance companies for financial strength. They are: AM Best (*www.ambest.com*), Moody's (*www.moodys.com*), Standard & Poor's (*www.standardandpoors.com*), and Duff & Phelps (*www.fitchrating.com*). Before you buy an insurance policy from any company, please be sure the company carries all of the following ratings: AM Best, A- or better; Moody's, AA or better; Standard & Poor's, AA or better; Duff & Phelps, AA or better. Don't settle for just one of these ratings. Insist upon seeing the ratings in print.

The first insurance agent I ever dealt with had a really high-pressure sales pitch. I'm still not sure if I bought

the right coverage. Are they all like that? My policies are up for renewal and I'm thinking about trying someone else.

Try another agent—someone who will be less impatient to make a sale. Remember, though, that you can't expect salespeople to take responsibility for your money; that's your job. I'm guessing, but it sounds as if you signed up the first time you visited the agent's office, no questions asked. Please take the time to read, compare, and question a number of policies. You shouldn't work with an agent who makes you feel bad for taking the time to do those things.

HEALTH INSURANCE

In recent years, private health insurance has become an increasingly complex and expensive item for all of us. At the same time, it is perhaps the most vital kind of insurance we can have. Without the proper health insurance, an illness or accident can wipe you out financially in a New York minute.

What would happen if I really needed medical care and I didn't have health insurance coverage?

Most hospitals (but not all!) would be obligated to care for you in an emergency, such as a car accident or a heart attack. But this care is not free. Ultimately you would be responsible for paying the medical bills, which could be substantial. One trip to the emergency room could put you and your family in debt for years.

But the perils go deeper. Without health insurance, you (and your children, if you have any) are statistically less likely to seek preventative care, such as an annual checkup, because you can't or won't want to pay for it out of your own pocket. As a result, any serious illness you may get is likely to be diagnosed late, which means that your treatment could be far more expensive and less effective.

Not having health insurance means, in short, that you could be deprived of the care you need and deserve—and still find yourself hundreds of thousands of dollars in debt. No matter what your age or state of health, protecting yourself with adequate medical insurance is an act of self-respect.

I just graduated from college and I'm on a tight budget while looking for a job and an apartment. I'm also healthy. Can't I do without health insurance until I can get coverage through my job?

No. In the first place, not all employers offer subsidized health coverage. Second, if they do offer it, you may have to wait three to six months to qualify for coverage. In the meantime, prudence apart, get used to taking responsibility for your health and finances. You'll find it liberating. Young as you are, and meager though your resources may be, health insurance is vitally important. No one can afford to take their health for granted. You might consider a short-term plan, often called a "gap" plan. It is designed to be low cost, can be issued quickly and provides coverage for up to a year.

There is so much talk in the news about health insurance that I am totally confused. What do I need to know to make a decision as to what type of coverage I should have?

Start by considering the following questions:

- How much can you comfortably pay in premiums and deductibles?

- Do you have a doctor whom you trust and depend on and want to keep seeing? Would he or she be available under the plan you are considering?
- Does anyone in your family have ongoing health-care needs? Does the plan cover the services he or she depends on, including specialists?

What sort of health insurance do most people have?

Sad to say, many Americans—about 41 million, including 12 million children—don't have any health insurance. They can't afford it, or believe they can't afford it. But of those Americans who do have health insurance, most are enrolled in the so-called "managed care" plans. What managed care means is that the insurance companies try to control—that is, "manage"—the costs of the medical care they're underwriting. Their most significant control mechanisms, from your point of view, are the following. First, they restrict your access to a list of doctors who accept the insurance companies' schedule of fees for whatever care you may need. (Your favorite doctor may or may not be among those on the list the plan provides.) Second, the companies require you to get a referral from your doctor—the one you've designated as your "primary care physician"—in order to see any specialist. Third, they require that the specialist also accept the insurance companies' fee schedule. Fourth, the company consults with—"second guesses" might be the more accurate phrase—your doctor on many procedures and tests that your doctor (or specialist) may consider necessary.

Are all managed care plans equally restrictive of my freedom of choice?

No, but the general rule is: the greater your freedom of choice, the higher the cost. The following are brief descriptions of the three principal types of managed care plans.

HMOs (Health Maintenance Organizations)

In general, HMOs are the least flexible health insurance policies. Premiums for these plans have gone up in recent years, in part because mandated benefits and pressure from consumers have made insurers more "generous" in giving access to the care you need. Despite the rising premiums, HMOs tend to be the least expensive form of health insurance. Copayments, when they are required at all, are usually small; and preventative care services are almost always covered. In exchange, you must see only approved doctors and will need to get permission from your primary care physician before you see specialists or seek alternative care.

PPOs (Preferred Provider Organizations)

A PPO gives you an incentive to stay within its network of doctors by covering more of your costs when you use a preferred provider. You may pay a flat copay or a percent of the fee for the services you receive. If you see providers who are not in the network it will generally cost you more, but you at least have the flexibility to see any doctor you like out of the network. PPOs usually allow you to see specialists without prior approval, but they do not always cover preventive care services and you will generally pay more out of pocket when you use services. PPO rules can be complex, so be sure to ask questions to learn what is and isn't covered before you buy this type of insurance.

POS (Point-of-Service) Plans

This is a type of flexible plan where you are encouraged to use network providers but are allowed to choose health-care providers outside your plan, usually at a higher copayment or deductible cost. The major difference between a POS plan and a regular PPO is that you can decide if you want to follow the HMO type "rules" and get your primary care doctor to refer you to specialists or pay more out of pocket by going to the providers of your choice without going through the referral process. It is called a point of service plan because you decide, at the point of service, to use it more like an HMO or PPO.

A Comparison

Which type of policy is the best?
There really isn't a single "best" policy. You should base your decision on your own needs and preferences, both financial and medical. Clearly, though, if your overriding concern is keeping access to your family doctor, and he or she isn't among the approved medical caregivers in any available HMO, you should go for a PPO or a POS, regardless of the extra cost. If cost is a big concern, then whichever of the managed care plans you choose, be aware that it will be cheaper if you buy it as part of a group—typically, a group of employees.

How do I get on a group health insurance plan?
If you're employed, you're usually eligible through your company, if it's large enough. You may also be eligible through some other membership organization such as a union. The policies offered are almost always of the managed care variety, which have been sold directly to the employer or organization and then made available to you. Group health insurance is what the majority of Americans have. It's cheaper than an individual policy because employers or organizations can often negotiate a lower rate and may subsidize part of the cost to eligible employees. They may also extend coverage to spouses, partners, and children of employees or members.

But what am I supposed to do if I'm self-employed, or unemployed, or work for a small business that doesn't offer a group plan?

You must buy individual health insurance from an insurance broker or company. Your best buy, if you're like most people and care a lot about costs as well as comprehensive coverage, is one of the managed care options: an HMO, a PPS, or a POS.

What if I'm on a really tight budget? How can I be safe on individual health insurance?

From a strictly financial point of view, you could think about purchasing catastrophic coverage. Catastrophic coverage pays for major medical and hospital expenses if you get seriously ill or injured. Premiums are lower on this type of insurance because you pay out of pocket for your usual expenses, such as checkups and even minor emergencies, and you will have a relatively high deductible if something major happens. Try to find a policy that is guaranteed renewable, has a maximum lifetime benefit of at least $1 million, and covers at least 80 percent of your doctor and hospital bills after you meet the deductible. Be cautious of plans that have caps on major expenses such as hospitalization. You may not realize the cost of care in your area and find yourself underinsured. Basically, with catastrophic insurance, you're betting that you will stay very healthy and that you will be able to pay for your basic preventative services. At the same time, you are protecting yourself from financial ruin if you should need substantial care.

Can't I get better coverage than that, for not too much more money?

That depends on what you mean by "too much." Ask about a base plan. There are many kinds of base plans that all generally cover most of your expenses when you need to stay in a hospital, when you have "medically necessary" surgery, when you visit a doctor, and when your doctor orders lab tests. The broadest—and most costly—of the base plans is indemnity insurance. It gives you the most freedom when picking doctors, treatments, and hospitals. Your insurance provider pays a fixed percentage of your doctors' charges, however large or small those charges are and whatever doctor you choose to see. But, again, you pay for this freedom with higher premiums. For some people the option of choosing any doctor they fancy is worth any expense. But beware: In some plans you will need to make up the difference between what your doctor charges and what the insurance company deems a "reasonable and customary" price for those services, even if you've already paid your (high) deductible.

Are there any ways to save money on an individual policy?

Here are two: First, some insurance companies offer discounts to people who are in good physical shape. Second, if you choose a high-deductible plan that meets IRS guidelines, you can set up your own health savings account (HSA) so that you'll be paying for your health insurance on a tax-deductible basis. HSA accounts can be used for dental, vision, and complementary medicine as well. Make sure the plan you choose is HSA compatible.

I've heard about these health savings accounts (HSAs). How do they work?

HSAs are accounts to which you can contribute money on a tax-deductible basis and then use the money later to pay your medical expenses. Any money that you don't use in a single year can be placed in an interest-bearing account and continue to grow with taxes deferred. These may be especially useful if you have a high deductible or copayment rate on your health insurance. For more information, go to *www.irs.ustreas.gov* and search for Publication 969, "Medical Savings Accounts."

I just started my own business and, so far, I am the only employee. Am I stuck buying individual health insurance?

It is actually possible to buy group health insurance for groups of one, although not all insurance companies or states allow this option and the specifics of the plans vary widely. One thing to keep in mind when considering this option is your own health. If it's poor, a group plan for one may be for you; such plans can't reject members for health reasons.

Once I have an individual policy, can I keep it forever?

It depends on your policy. Guaranteed renewable policies can be kept forever, as long as you pay your premiums on time (although the insurance company can raise your premiums). Optionally renewable policies usually allow the insurance company to stop your coverage, but only within specific time periods, such as the anniversary date of the policy. Conditionally renewable policies can be terminated by the insurance company for certain specific reasons (such as if you are covered under a group plan at work and you retire), but not if your health becomes poor. If your policy is optionally or conditionally renewable, check to see if your insurer is required to inform you when it is about to expire, and whether you have an option to convert the policy to individual or individual family coverage.

The insurance policy I'm considering has a stop-loss provision. What does that mean?

Although most major medical policies require you to make copayments, they typically limit the total amount you would have to pay within a given period of time, usually a year. That limit is the stop-loss figure, and it varies by company and policy. If your stop-loss is $3,000 per year, you will never have to pay more than $3,000 (in addition to your premiums); after you have paid $3,000, the insurance company will pay 100 percent of your covered expenses. Consider stop-loss provisions when you are comparing policies.

What's the difference between health insurance continuations and conversions?

In certain circumstances, your eligibility for your insurance plan may change (for example, if you lose your job or begin working part-time; if you are widowed, divorced, or separated from your insured spouse; or if you are too old to be covered under your parents' insurance, etc.). Both federal and state laws almost always require, in these types of circumstances, that you be given an opportunity to continue or convert your health insurance policy. Continuation means that you can keep the coverage, often at your own expense, for a specific period of time. Conversion means you have the option of converting your group coverage to individual (or individual family) coverage.

COBRA

If I have group insurance through my employer and I lose my job, will I automatically lose my health insurance and have to buy an individual policy?

Not right away. The Consolidated Omnibus Budget Reconciliation Act of 1985 (COBRA) requires most employers with 20 or more employees to give you the opportunity to continue your health insurance for up to 18 months, at your expense. Your employer can charge you up to 102 percent of its cost of your insurance—which sounds like a lot and is almost certainly more than you were paying in premiums before, but still might be cheaper than buying your own individual policy.

How do I know if I'm eligible for COBRA?
You are eligible for COBRA coverage in a number of different circumstances, including: you lose your job; you quit your job; your spouse who was the primary insured member of your family dies; your child is no longer a minor; you are getting divorced from a spouse who is the primary insured member; or you begin working part-time. These are called qualifying events. You are not eligible if you work for the federal government, in the District of Columbia, or for an employer with less than 20 workers. (If you work for a small business, you might be eligible to continue your health insurance anyway, depending on the state in which you live. Check with your state's department of insurance.)

I work full time and I'm pregnant. After the baby is born I would like to work part time for a while. As long as I'm still working for the same employer, why would I need COBRA?
Because you usually need to work a minimum number of hours per week, often more than half of a normal workweek, in order to qualify for your employer's medical plan. The extra cost of COBRA, to you, is something to keep in mind if you decide to try to work out a part-time schedule with your employer.

My sister works for a small restaurant in town with only 12 employees, so the owner offers health insur-

ance that isn't subject to COBRA. What are her options if she loses her job?

Many states require all employers to offer you the opportunity to convert to an individual policy, but the coverage may be more limited than what your sister had under the group plan, and the premiums may be higher. Call the department of insurance in your state to see if she will at least have this option.

How long can I keep my health coverage under COBRA?

Usually for no more than 18 months. However, your coverage can be extended for up to 36 months under certain extenuating circumstances, such as if the primary insured person dies. If you become eligible for Medicare (which makes you automatically ineligible for COBRA coverage), but your spouse isn't eligible for Medicare, your spouse can extend his or her COBRA coverage for up to 36 months.

What if I become disabled while I have insurance coverage under COBRA?

You may be able to extend your COBRA coverage for up to 29 months, but your premiums will rise for those additional months, depending on your particular situation.

I'm about to get laid off. I had great coverage with my employer's plan, but it's going to cost a lot to keep it up under COBRA. Can I opt for one of the COBRA versions of the less comprehensive, cheaper plans that my company offers?

No. Your coverage under COBRA must be the same as the coverage you had before you were laid off. Your employer might permit you to drop certain types of coverage, like your vision care. That could save you some money, but your employer is not required to help you.

My husband and I are both self-employed, so we share an individual health insurance policy. Now we're getting divorced. How do we decide who gets to keep it?
Here's one decision you don't have to make. Neither of you can keep a shared individual policy. You must each reenroll at the company as individuals, or you can choose to go to different insurance companies.

I don't ever want to worry about my children's health care. Both my husband and I have health insurance. Shouldn't we play it safe and add our children to both plans?
You could, but it really doesn't make sense. If one or both of your plans are individual, it's going to cost a lot of extra money to cover your kids on two plans. Similarly, group plans charge more for family coverage and tend to offer similar preventative care services. If you compare your two plans, you may find that you won't be getting much, if any, additional coverage by signing the kids up for both. It'd be far better to take that extra money and invest it for growth. Alternatively, buy a separate policy for the children, so they'll be covered in the event of your job loss.

COBRA coverage costs so much money! Is it really the right thing for me?
If you're in good health, you may be able to find a better deal than paying COBRA premiums, if you're willing to do the research. But make sure that you compare services, not just prices.

I'm in such poor health that I'm afraid I won't be able to get health insurance. Is there anything I can do?
High-risk health insurance pools guarantee health insurance to

all individuals, no matter how sick they may already be. While pools vary from state to state, they are generally operated by an association of all health insurance companies doing business in a state. These companies are not providing coverage out of the goodness of their hearts. They have been required by the government to offer coverage to state residents who have either been rejected by other insurers for similar coverage or are insured at a higher premium or with more severe restrictions than they would be under the pool. These pools are not perfect—premiums are often high and the benefits may not be adequate to meet your needs—but they do offer an insurance alternative for people in poor health. Call your state insurance department.

Medicare, Medicaid, and Medigap

As of the year 2004, approximately 13 percent of Americans were age 65 and older. By the year 2050, 22 percent of Americans will be over age 65. No wonder health care for the elderly is a serious political issue.

And it's serious not only because of the size of the elderly population. For many of us, the crux of the matter is this: Just when we go on fixed incomes and no longer have funds available to pay for private medical insurance, our medical needs and costs are likely to go up—sometimes way up. This is when Medicare and Medicaid will come in to save the day.

That's the idea, anyway. But these are difficult times in which to grow old in America. Our whole scheme of social insurance—the famed "safety net" of Social Security, federal disability insurance, unemployment insurance, Medicare,

Medicaid, and other federal programs—is under great stress. The main reason is the ballooning elderly population. The withholding taxes younger Americans pay are used to support the current retired generation, which is still a relatively small group. But as retired Americans become a huge group, and as the working, withholding-tax-paying population becomes a relatively small one, the painful question arises: Who is going to make up for the shortfall in support for the safety net? The problem is not just financial; it's also intensely ideological. There are conflicting views as to how much of the support should continue to be shouldered by society as a right and responsibility of membership in that society, and how much should be borne by the individuals who are growing old.

The problem will not be solved easily or quickly. We will have plenty of opportunities to follow proposed solutions as they're being discussed—indeed, to influence them with our votes. But big changes are already upon us. Job security has been a nostalgic dream for some time, as employees who expected to be working at the same job until retirement are now routinely laid off ("reengineered" or "downsized"), their places given to younger workers who may or may not be technologically more clever but are certainly cheaper. For many older Americans, full Social Security still kicks in at 65, with average benefits of $12,528 per year, but we are already seeing benefits reduced for younger Americans; anyone born after 1959 qualifies for full benefits at age 67.

In what follows I'm going to focus on the most insurance-like social programs—Medicare, Medicaid, and Medigap insurance, a private supplement to Medicare.

Medicare Coverage

What is Medicare?

Medicare is the largest federal health insurance program, and it is the major health insurer for Americans over age 65 and Americans who are disabled. Once you qualify, you can use Original Medicare, which is a traditional fee-for-service health plan, or, in many cases, you can use a managed care organization—an HMO or a PPO that contracts with Medicare.

What does Medicare cover?

There are free services in each state that will help you understand the details of Medicare eligibility and coverage. Very briefly, if you are 65 or older, you can get a certain amount of coverage for hospital and doctor visits from Medicare. The type of coverage Medicare offers depends on whether you are covered by Medicare Part A, Part B, or both.

Medicare Part A

If you qualify for Social Security you are automatically covered by Medicare Part A. In most cases there is no premium charge to you for this coverage because part of the Social Security tax you paid while you were working went toward this coverage.

Part A generally covers inpatient-type benefits such as:

- Hospital care
- Skilled nursing facility
- Home health care
- Hospice care

Medicare Part B

Medicare Part B coverage is automatic, but it is *voluntary* coverage from which you can opt out and for which a monthly premium, currently about $45 a month, will be charged. This monthly premium is commonly deducted from your Social Security check.

Part B provides for:

- Physician's services
- Outpatient hospital care
- Physical therapy and the use of medical equipment
- Ambulance expenses

Note: Neither of these policies provides coverage for dental care, vision care, or, as of this writing, prescription drugs.

So I don't have to do anything to purchase Part B?
No. When you become eligible for Part A benefits, you will be sent an enrollment form for Part B, but you should fill it out only if you want to *reject* the coverage. If you fail to reject coverage within two months from the date you received the form, you will be automatically enrolled in Part B. If you opt out of Part B you can enroll later at any time, but at a higher cost to you.

What percentage of my medical bills does Part B cover?
It normally covers 80 percent of the approved charges for covered expenses, subject to a calendar year deductible of $110.

What do you mean by approved charges?
The approved charge is the lesser of the actual charge or the amount indicated in Medicare's annual fee schedule.

Do you have to be over 65 to receive Medicare?

Not necessarily. You are also eligible for Medicare at any age if you have qualified for Social Security Disability Insurance for any reason—such as, for example, if you've developed permanent kidney failure.

How do I get Medicare and when do benefits begin?

Once you apply for and begin receiving your Social Security benefits, you will automatically be eligible for Medicare when you turn 65. Coverage begins on the first day of the month in which you turn 65. When you are covered, a Medicare card will be issued to you.

If I am over 65 and need to go into a nursing home, Medicare will automatically pay for it, right?

No—this is a huge and costly misunderstanding that many people share. Not only does Medicare not automatically pick up your nursing care costs as a senior citizen, it will almost *never* cover them. Medicare has very limited coverage for long-term care. It is usually only available if you are in an acute-care hospital for three days before entering a "skilled nursing facility"—a facility that must be Medicare-certified—and Medicare must define the type of care you need as "skilled" medical care, not custodial care. Custodial care is what 99.5 percent of the people in nursing facilities receive; only about 0.5 percent of the people in nursing homes receive skilled care. Even if your care falls under this 0.5 percent, you are only covered for reasonable and customary expenses for the first 20 days; for the next 80 days you are required to pay about $124 a day and Medicare covers the remaining reasonable and customary expenses. After those first 100 days, you are on your own no matter what. The bottom line is that Medicare rarely pays for nursing home costs.

If Medicare won't pay for me to stay in a nursing home, will it pay for my care at home?

Possibly, in a very limited number of cases. If a doctor certifies that you need to be cared for at home by a part-time or full-time skilled nurse, speech therapist, or physical therapist, and the provider is Medicare-certified, you might receive some coverage. But be aware that very few situations qualify under these conditions.

My father still lives at home but he had a stroke last year and needs a lot of assistance, including physical therapy. What can he expect Medicare to pay for?

Because he needs physical therapy, Medicare will cover some of his expenses. But usually, if you are capable of living at home, Medicare will pay only if your doctor certifies that you need very particular occasional skilled assistance, such as physical therapy or speech therapy, and that you will improve with such treatment.

My father really needs help at home with things like cleaning and cooking, since he can't stand up for long periods of time. Will Medicare cover these services temporarily, as he should be able to do them again once he recovers?

No. Even if your father's nonmedical needs are related to an injury, Medicare will not pay for home health care. He needs long-term care insurance for this. Long-term care insurance covers care he receives in an adult day care center, continuing care retirement communities, and assisted living facilities. It will increase his premiums to have all these types of facilities covered, but if he has the protection, he will have more flexibility in seeking care later.

My mother needs to go into a nursing home. What kind of skilled nursing care will Medicare pay for?
Not very much. If she has been hospitalized for at least three consecutive days within the last 30 days and if she will be receiving skilled nursing care in a certified facility, Medicare will pay for the reasonable and customary costs of the first 20 days and part of the cost (less her copayment) for the following 80 days of her stay.

What if she can't afford those copayments?
If she has Medigap Plan C insurance (discussed later in this book), it will pay for the copayments between the 21st and 100th day of her stay, if Medicare approves her stay.

What if she has to stay longer than 100 days?
She will have to pay out of her own pocket. This is when long-term care coverage becomes essential.

Does Medicare pay for any nursing services, ever?
Yes, when you're dying, Medicare will pay for a portion of hospice care. A caregiver is provided to ease the pain and suffering of the patient and his or her family during their last days together, and it will not matter whether you need the services at home or in a facility.

MEDICARE PART D

I keep hearing about Medicare Part D; do I need this?
Medicare D is the new prescription drug plan. If you already have a Medigap policy with drug coverage you may be able to keep that coverage. If not, a Medicare D policy will provide you with the prescription drug coverage. For the best rates, enroll in a Medicare Part D plan when you become eligible for Medicare. The website, www.medicare.gov, has tools to help you figure out the best option for your situation.

MEDIGAP COVERAGE

Can you explain Medigap insurance?

As you can see, Medicare will not cover all your medical costs. Also, like other health insurers, Medicare will require you to pay deductibles in order to receive your benefits. Therefore, you may want to buy additional coverage to protect you from having to spend a lot of money on these fees. Medigap is a type of insurance policy designed by private insurers to supplement Medicare coverage (although it does not cover long-term care). There are many different types of Medigap policies and they vary in quality and cost.

How do I know which Medigap policy to purchase?

The standard policies are referred to as plans A through J. A is the most basic (and least expensive) and generally as you move through the alphabet, the number of benefits expands to J, which is a more comprehensive and more expensive supplement. Just so you know, any insurance company that sells Medigap coverage is required to offer plan A, with the basic benefits.

The most popular plan is C. You will need to decide which policy is right for you, but if you purchase Medigap, look for a policy that covers at least a 20 percent coinsurance cost for doctor bills, hospital and doctor visit deductibles, excess doctor fees, and preventative care. Don't ever buy more than one of these policies, because they expand on one another, so you would be paying twice for some benefits.

Here are the basic features of each plan:

- Plan A pays the coinsurance required by Medicare Part A for the 61st through the 90th day that you are hospitalized in each benefit period and for the 60 nonrenewable lifetime hospitalization inpatient reserve days that you can use to extend your coverage; up to one year (over your lifetime) of your eligible hospital expenses after Medicare benefits have been used; the first three pints of blood you need each year; and the Part B coinsurance after your annual deductible is paid.

- Plan B includes everything in Plan A, plus it picks up the inpatient hospital deductible that Medicare Part A requires.
- Plan C includes everything listed above in plans A and B, and pays for the coinsurance in a skilled nursing care facility during days 21 through 100 in each benefit period; the deductible required by Medicare Part B; and most of your medically necessary emergency care in a foreign country.
- Plan D covers everything listed above for plans A through C, *except* the deductible required by Medicare Part B, and includes a benefit of up to $1,600 per year for services you would need at home on a short-term basis if you were recovering from illness, injury, or surgery.
- Plan E covers everything listed above for plans A through C, *except* the deductible required by Medicare Part B, and includes coverage for up to $120 per year for preventative care, such as flu shots, cholesterol tests, or annual checkups.
- Plan F covers everything listed above for plans A through C, plus 100 percent of any fees you would be required to pay as excess charges under Medicare Part B.
- Plan G covers everything listed above for plans A through C, and pays 80 percent of the excess charge fees described in Plan F. Plan G also includes coverage for "at-home recovery"—that is, authorized care you might receive in your home, such as assistance with bathing, once you've been released from the hospital.

- Plan H covers everything listed above for plans A through C, *except* the deductible required by Medicare Part B.
- Plan I covers everything listed above for plan E, plus the excess charges benefit in plan F, at-home recovery as in Plan G.
- Plan J includes every benefit listed above, *except* that it covers 100 percent of your excess charges (as in plan F, rather than the 80 percent coverage for this fee in plan G).

Will a Medigap policy cover any home or long-term health-care needs?

In certain limited circumstances, Medigap may cover some home health-care services but, as you can see, even the most comprehensive Medigap policy will not cover long-term care costs. Remember, the care must be Medicare-approved in order for the Medigap policy to kick in.

If Medigap policies are standardized, why do different insurance companies charge different amounts of money for the same policies?

There are many different reasons for this, including the laws of the state you are in and the way the company calculates its premiums. It is absolutely worth your while to compare prices, and it is quite easy to do this because you know that the terms of the policies are the same: A plan C from one company should offer the exact same benefits as a plan C from another company, no matter where you live.

Does everyone need Medigap?

Not necessarily. And it may not always be the best buy, even if you decide that you need some supplemental insurance. For example, you may be eligible to participate in some group health coverage through the employer you had before you retired.

Can I be turned down for Medigap coverage if I am in poor health?

This is an important point. When you qualify for Original Medicare Part B, you have a six-month open enrollment period during which you can buy any Medigap policy offered in your state, no matter what your health status is. This is the best time to decide whether you want to make Medigap part of your insurance coverage.

My neighbor has part of her Social Security check paid directly to a company, which she says she uses instead of Medigap. Can you tell me more about this?

She most likely is talking about what is known as a Managed Care Organization.

MANAGED CARE ORGANIZATIONS

What is a managed care organization?

A managed care organization (MCO) works like an HMO, as follows: The organization you have selected becomes the recipient of the premium that you have been paying out of your Social Security check. In exchange for that fixed monthly payment from the Medicare program, the provider you have chosen will take care of your medical needs. This usually offers you a savings and broader benefits than what you would get on your own. Some HMOs and MCOs do not charge anything beyond the Medicare premiums, and some charge more but offer more services as well. Some companies offer additional benefits and therefore eliminate the need for Medigap insurance. Getting coverage via an MCO or HMO is, in my opinion, the preferred way to go because, in general, you can be sufficiently covered at a far lower cost than through Medigap.

How do I choose a good MCO?

Please take the time to investigate as many plans as you can, but no less than two plans offered in your area. When you do, be sure to compare the following features:

- *Cost of care.* Although many MCOs do not charge premiums beyond the amounts you are currently paying to Medicare, some do. Check what your potential plan covers and how much it will cost you. Is it a bare-bones plan, meaning that it offers the minimum coverage required by Medicare? Are you willing to pay a slightly higher premium for broader coverage? Please pay attention when comparing potential out-of-pocket costs by looking at the deductibles and the copayments each plan requires.
- *Type of coverage and optional benefits.*
- *Choice of providers.* Many of you prefer to choose your own doctors, but you may not be able to do so if you choose an MCO that requires you to use its network. The MCOs that do not restrict your choice of doctors are known as Medicare PPOs, or open-ended HMOs. Be clear on this point ahead of time, so that after you have enrolled you are not surprised to learn that you cannot see your regular doctor.
- *Quality of care.* Find out if your MCO encourages preventive care by paying for some of those services. There are many nonprofit groups that monitor the quality of care that particular MCOs provide. *Consumer Reports* has done some comparisons of Medigap plans and HMOs, so you may want to consult a *Consumer Reports* index before buying.

What are the main advantages of an MCO?

The most significant advantage is the opportunity to obtain

full Medicare coverage, either Part A or Part B, at a lower cost. Additional benefits may also exist, such as services and supplies that are not usually covered by Medicare. A good MCO that offers additional benefits could eliminate the need for Medigap insurance or Medicare supplemental insurance, saving you even more money. Usually, paperwork is reduced as well because in most cases no claims need be submitted since all benefits are provided through the MCO network.

What are the disadvantages of MCOs?

The primary disadvantage could be the restricted choice of physicians. Remember, many MCOs require you to use network doctors and hospitals; if a wider choice is allowed, you may incur higher deductibles and copayments when using non-network providers, just like a regular POS or PPO. It is also possible that the emphasis on cost could lead to a declining level of care in the MCO environment in the future, if doctors are pressured to contain costs and handle larger caseloads.

Given the advantages versus the disadvantages, which way do you think I should go?

This will depend on the options available under the individual plan in your area but, on the whole, I would consider going the MCO route if the plan that you are being offered is a good one that gives you access to the doctors you like.

MEDICAID

Medicaid (which is called MediCal in California) is a combined federal and state welfare program that covers medical care for poor Americans (and about 40 percent of all the people who are in nursing homes today). In order to qualify for Medicaid, you must be poor or medically needy, over age 65 or under age 21, blind, disabled, or receiving certain welfare benefits.

I've heard of people trying to "qualify" for Medicaid in a nursing home by putting everything into their children's names. Isn't this financially risky?

It is definitely risky, and not only financially. A major risk is that people on Medicaid have very limited control over their (also limited) medical options. Also, when parents sign over all their resources to their children, they become completely dependent. That can be emotionally and financially unhealthy for everyone involved. Finally, depending on the value of the assets transferred, there can be significant negative tax consequences for your children. Please consult with a qualified elder-law attorney before you transfer any assets or make any decisions. It may not be worth it!

My wife needs to go into a nursing home. How do I know if she will qualify for Medicaid?

It can be frustrating to sort through the rules concerning Medicaid, which change frequently and vary from state to state. Generally, your wife will have to have a doctor certify that she needs the specific kind of care that nursing homes provide. She will also need to be living in a state that provides the relevant Medicaid benefits; be at least 65 years old, disabled, or blind; and have only a limited amount of income and assets. If you find yourself in this situation, seek the assistance of an attorney who specializes in elder-care law in your state or contact your local office on aging, which may be under the aegis of the state health department.

I would like to move from New York to Virginia, to be in a nursing home near my daughter. How do I establish Virginia's residency qualifications?

Just move to Virginia and plan to stay there indefinitely. As long as you're in the state and have no plans to leave, you are considered a resident and should be immediately eligible for Medicaid. But just to be sure, check out the state's eligibility requirements at *www.Medicaid.com/medicaid.*

What are the financial requirements for Medicaid? How much income can I have and still qualify for Medicaid coverage in a nursing home?

If you are single, everything counts. That means that all your income (earned or unearned) is taken into consideration in determining whether you qualify. This includes your Social Security, alimony, pension, worker's compensation, annuities, unemployment, interest, gifts, and dividends.

As of the year 2001, in 33 states there is no limit on the amount of income you can have before qualifying for Medicaid. If you live in one of these states, you will qualify for Medicaid if the monthly cost of a nursing home stay will be more expensive than your monthly income. The other 17 states require that your income be below a set limit, which varies by state. If you live in one of these states, make sure you have a financial adviser with a specialty in elder-care law who can help you sort things out: Alabama, Alaska, Arizona, Arkansas, Colorado, Delaware, Florida, Idaho, Iowa, Louisiana, Mississippi, Nevada, New Jersey, New Mexico, Oklahoma, South Dakota, and Texas.

As an unmarried person, what other assets can I have and still qualify for Medicaid coverage of my nursing home stay?

Most unmarried people must turn over almost all their assets to the nursing home in order to have Medicaid pay their bill. However, most states will allow you to keep your house if you'll most likely be able to return there or if a member of your immediate family is living there at the time you apply for coverage. You can often keep your car, no matter what it is worth, if you use it to receive medical care. Otherwise, you can only keep a car that is worth less than $4,500 and investments up to about $2,000.

This is only the most general information. There are a lot of other rules about what you can and cannot keep, but the bottom line is that as an unmarried person you must give up almost everything you have worked so hard to accumulate in order to qualify for Medicaid coverage in a nursing home. Unmarried and married persons should each get legal advice as to the available options regarding assets.

As a married person, how do I determine if I qualify for Medicaid?

Again, rules for married people vary from state to state. In community-property states (Arizona, California, Idaho, Louisiana, Nevada, New Mexico, Texas, Washington, and Wisconsin), all of your income from any source, no matter which spouse the checks are made out to, is considered to be equally divided between both of you. So if you live in one of these states, half of all the income you and your spouse have is considered yours, even if, for example, most of it comes from your spouse's pension.

In any other state, only checks that are made out to you count toward your Medicaid eligibility. In other words, if you get a Social Security check made out only to you, Medicaid considers it to belong only to you, even if you normally deposit it in a joint bank account with your spouse. If you receive dividends or interest on an account with both your names on it, that money is considered to be evenly split between the two of you.

As is true for single people in most states, if the cost of a nursing home is higher than your income, you will qualify for the Medicaid nursing home funds. If you live in one of the 17 states with the set limit, you will need to fall below that cap. An elder-care attorney can help you figure this out.

Once I qualify, what happens to my healthy spouse?
He or she will be given a basic living allowance, a generally modest amount of money that doesn't have to go toward the nursing home, to make sure that he or she is not totally impoverished. Your elder-care specialist can help you estimate the amount that your stay-at-home spouse would be able to keep—or even have the amount increased according to his or her needs—because it will be completely different in each state, as are the formulas that determine it.

Do married people also have an asset eligibility test?
Yes, after qualifying on the income test, you also need to pass an asset eligibility test. Your home, car, and personal property are generally protected for your healthy spouse. Married couples can also keep some money in investments or cash: usually about $80,000, which sounds like a lot, but remember, this is all the stay-at-home spouse will have, aside from his or her income, which has basically just been cut in half. You can see that you have to lose most of your assets in order to qualify.

Studies of individuals entering nursing homes have documented that half of the people in the study on Medicaid were not poor when they entered the facility. They had to "spend down" their assets until nothing was left before Medicaid took over.

Is it true that even if I qualify for Medicaid, the state can put a lien against my property after I die?

Actually, yes. The 1993 OBRA (Omnibus Budget Reconciliation Act) requires any state that receives funds for Medicaid to have a recovery plan in place. More and more states, in fact, are actively starting to recoup Medicaid expenses. What's more, your family or other beneficiaries will have to pay despite the fact that there is no way to prove that the amount of money Medicaid is seeking from your estate was actually spent on you. So please be careful here and get advice from an elder-care specialist.

But you said that the house I lived in with my wife is exempt from such recouping efforts! I mean, she's not suddenly going to find herself homeless, is she?

No, she won't. Generally, while your spouse is living in the house they will not try to take it. Once your spouse dies, however, and the estate is left to her beneficiaries, the state could try to make a claim against it. Your wife should consider revising her estate plan so your heirs don't end up losing their share of the house and other assets.

Can I just give my money to my kids and then apply for Medicaid?

Please don't do this! Medicaid is a form of public assistance, and all types of public assistance make you liable for prosecution if you lie on your application or knowingly defraud the program. The government can look back in time to see whether you have given away money to anyone, including your children or any other relatives, in the past 36 months. If you give away your assets in order to get Medicaid benefits primarily to pay for your care in a nursing home, you may be making yourself vulnerable to this type of accusation and, if you are found to have knowingly defrauded the program, you may become ineligible for Medicaid benefits for a period of time and possibly be accused of fraud. Further, any professional financial advisers who recommend that you do this could be sent to jail or fined. Beyond the illegalities of such actions lie the more personal issues of the effect asset transfers have on your autonomy and your family.

So if I give my assets to my children and get caught, how long do I have to wait before I can apply for Medicaid again?

The length of time you can be barred from Medicaid depends on how much money you gave away. The state takes an average-per-month cost of what nursing homes charge in your area and divides that monthly figure into the value of the assets you gave away. So let's say you gave $200,000 worth of assets, and the average price of a nursing home near you is $5,000 a month. Dividing the first figure into the second yields 40, which means that you'll be barred from eligibility for 40 months.

What if I give away stocks? Is that the same as giving away money?

Of course. An asset is an asset. It won't work, either, to put the stock in a living revocable trust. That will extend your noneligibility to 60 months—five years.

If I don't want to apply for Medicaid but I have worked out a good combination of Medicare and Medigap coverage, can I rest easy?

Medicare and Medigap will certainly cover some of your needs, but if you really want to know that you have taken care of potential nursing home costs, you need to purchase long-term care insurance.

LONG-TERM CARE INSURANCE

For a society that's growing older by the minute, we're not providing very well for our old age. We expect individuals and families to do it mostly on their own. But even as individuals and families, we seem to be in denial about what's happening to us. Nowhere is this more obvious than with respect to long-term care insurance—perhaps the most essential kind of insurance—which many of us will need when we are old. Long-term care will be a fact of life for most of us, so let's face it here and now. Having done so, you will, I hope, go on to buy this kind of protection.

What is long-term care?

This is any type of medical, social, or support service you may need over an extended period of time. Elderly or chronically ill people may eventually need help bathing, dressing, taking medicine, shopping, doing laundry, cleaning, or getting around outside. These services can be extremely expensive and, in most circumstances, Medicare, Medicaid, and Medigap will not pay for them.

What are my chances of needing long-term care?

The frightening reality is that after age 65, most people have a 50-50 chance of needing long-term care. The odds of needing such care are higher than the odds of your house burning down or of your getting into a serious car accident. You are covered for those possibilities, aren't you? Well, the average age at which people enter a nursing home is 84 years and the average stay is two years and nine months. As of 2004, that's going to cost anywhere from $5,000 to $10,000 a month—a lot of money if you have to pay out of your own pocket.

I took care of my kids when they were young, and I expect them to take care of me when I am older. What's wrong with that?

Nothing. Many adult children do take care of their parents. Younger family members (usually the women) provide 70 to 80 percent of all home health care and long-term care for their elders. However, there are enormous financial, emotional, and psychological costs when families have to maintain an intensive level of care over an extended period of time. Long-term care insurance doesn't mean your children can't, or won't, care for you, but it does ensure that you will not be placing a financial burden on your family at a time when they will already be under considerable stress.

Doesn't standard health insurance offer long-term care benefits?

Typically, no, it doesn't. And when it does, the benefits are limited.

But I've heard long-term care insurance is very expensive.

If you think long-term care insurance is expensive, you should compare it to the cost of a nursing home stay. Let's say you are 55 and will need to be in a nursing home at age 84: The projected yearly cost of a nursing home 30 years from now, if you live in middle America (assuming an annual rate of inflation of 5 percent), would be approximately $148,000. Given that the average nursing home stay is two years and nine months, that would mean a total cost to you of about $671,000. The total cost of a top-notch long-term care (LTC) policy, if you started it at the age of 55 and paid each year until you were 84, would be $81,600. Look at the numbers: You will pay more than 8.2 times as much for the total cost of a nursing home stay (that is, if you only stay two years and nine months) as you did for all your LTC premiums. (This assumes that there were no increases in premiums and that you did not invest the premium money over those years.) Please note: In the year 2006, a stay in a nursing home in the metropolitan New York area was already above $130,000 a year. For you New Yorkers, think about what that cost will be in 30 years!

But why should I buy it, if I take good care of myself?
Don't we all buy insurance in the hope that we will never need it? As I said, you are more likely to use your long-term care insurance policy than you are to use your fire or car insurance policy. One in 1,200 people will use their fire insurance, one in 248 people will use their car insurance, but one in two people who have long-term care insurance will use it, and it is the one insurance that you most likely do not have.

Should my marital status affect my decision about whether to purchase this insurance?
Everyone has to make the decision that's best for them, but here are some things to keep in mind: When you have to go into an assisted-living center or a nursing home and are leaving a healthy spouse behind, it is critical that he or she still have the means to live. Price a couple of nursing homes in your area and ask yourself what would happen to your partner if she had to pay those bills and support herself at the same time. Most of us would be financially devastated. Now, if you are single and no one will be hurt if you need to use all your income and assets to pay for nursing-home care, that's one

thing. But do you have children whom you want to provide for after your death? Charities you want to give to? Finally, is spending it all on a nursing home what you want to do with the money you have worked so hard for? That said, be sure that you and your partner will be able to comfortably afford those premiums, even after you are both retired. Otherwise, don't buy the policy.

Is long-term care insurance tax-deductible?

As of January 1997, if you purchase a long-term care policy that meets certain definitions established by the Health Insurance Portability and Accountability Act of 1996, your premiums, within certain limits, can be itemized as a tax deduction for medical expenses. These are called tax-qualified policies. Ask your accountant or an attorney or financial planner with an elder-care specialty about whether the policy you are considering would qualify. But remember: Your premiums, along with other out-of-pocket deductible medical expenses, will have to be in excess of 7.5 percent of your adjusted gross income to qualify for a deduction.

Long-term care insurance is a subject of much interest today, and in the future, you'll be hearing more about the issue of tax deductibility. Beginning in 1997, corporations have been able to pay for long-term care insurance coverage for their employees and take the cost of the premiums as a business expense for the company. This employer-paid long-term care insurance is not taxable to the employee. For the self-employed, long-term care insurance is now a deductible business expense. There have also been proposals for long-term care insurance premiums to become completely tax-deductible and for people to be able to buy long-term care insurance with the money already put away in their retirement accounts. Keep an eye out for more news about this topic.

What's the difference between a non-tax-qualified policy and a tax-qualified policy?

One big difference is that, with a tax-qualified plan (TQ), your long-term care insurance premiums may be tax deductible, as described above. With a non-tax-qualified plan (NTQ)—which has become less widely available in recent years—you may not get the tax deduction. The other major difference is in what triggers the benefits in a TQ versus an NTQ policy. This is called "making it through the gatekeepers."

If you have a TQ plan—which is fast becoming the most common type of plan—in order to make it through the gatekeepers, you must generally meet one of the two conditions that follow.

The first condition is not to be able to perform certain *activities of daily living (ADLs)*. In order to function normally, most of us need to be able to (1) feed ourselves; (2) clothe ourselves; (3) transfer ourselves (get in and out of bed, chairs, and the like, unattended); (4) be continent; (5) use the toilet; and (6) bathe ourselves. With a good TQ policy, if you got to a point in your life where you could not perform *any two* of the qualifying ADLs without substantial assistance, then you would qualify for benefits.

The second condition is *cognitive impairment*, which simply means that you qualify if you come down with, say, Alzheimer's disease or cannot think or act clearly and therefore become a danger to yourself or others.

In NTQ plans, you can usually claim your benefits with a different condition, which is known as *medical necessity*. This is where a doctor certifies that it is medically necessary for you to have long-term care—for example, if you are unstable and in danger of falling. This is a good gatekeeper to have in your policy, since it is generally easier to satisfy than the two-ADL gatekeeper. But again, it is becoming less widely available.

In the past, I have always preferred NTQ policies. But as said, today many insurance companies are no longer offering NTQ plans. As well, the government has stated that the benefits you receive in an NTQ plan could be taxed as income, so if you ever used the benefits, you might have to pay taxes on them (although most likely you would have at least a partial offset for deductible medical expenses). Also, NTQ premiums tend to be a little higher—about 5 percent. Meanwhile, benefits from a TQ plan can definitely be received income-tax free. Based on all this, a tax-qualified plan is probably the better, safer way to go.

If you do buy an NTQ policy, be sure that the insurance company will allow you to convert your policy to a TQ policy any time you want to, without new underwriting. Check the policy carefully for this, and make sure that if you do convert the policy at some future date, the company will base your new premium on your original age of entry into your former (NTQ) policy.

How do I know if I can afford to buy an LTC policy?

If you are not able to pay your bills or are just making ends meet each month, long-term care insurance is certainly not for you. But if you are able to save some of your income each month after your expenses, and you have liquid assets of at least $50,000 and own your home, then long-term care insurance may be worthwhile for you. The key thing is to be absolutely sure that you will be able to pay your premiums once you are retired.

Ask yourself the following questions:

- Could you keep this policy if your premiums increased by 20 percent?
- Do you expect your income to increase or decrease in

the next 10 years? If it decreases, will you be able to keep the policy in effect?

- How will you pay the premiums—from savings, from income, or will your family pay them for you?

Long-term care insurance is meant to help keep you from going into the poorhouse in case of the need for long-term care, not to put you in the poorhouse while you are paying for the insurance. It will do no good to buy a policy at age 55, retire at age 65, and then, at age 75, find that you can no longer afford the premiums. No matter how long you've paid into a policy, in most policies once you stop paying you'll no longer be covered. If you think you may not be able to afford your coverage in later years, you would be better off not to purchase the insurance in the first place, and to invest the money instead.

I'm only in my 50s. If the average age of entry into a nursing home is 84, shouldn't I wait until I am about 80 to buy LTC insurance?

Please don't. By then, the cost may become prohibitive. Not only that, your health may prevent you from being able to qualify for it. As with all insurance policies, you have to meet certain health requirements in order to purchase an LTC policy.

What is the optimal age to buy long-term care insurance?

I would say the optimal age is about 59, as long as you are sure that you're going to be able to make those payments when you're 74 and beyond. Remember, these premiums should not make daily living difficult for you and your spouse, now or after your retirement.

I am currently 50 years old and my agent says it is the perfect time to buy an LTC policy, but I have heard you say one should wait until age 59. Why?

Two reasons. First, by age 59 I believe that most people have a clear outlook on their financial future and know what they will be able to afford when they no longer have a paycheck coming in.

As of the writing of this book, at 50 the cost of a good policy with appropriate benefit levels is about $2,300 a year. Are you sure that you know beyond a shadow of a doubt that you will be able to afford $2,300 a year for the rest of your life? For most people, I don't think so. And nothing would be less useful than for you to have paid $2,300 a year for 20 or 25 years and then have something happen that causes you to drop the policy just when you might need it. At the age of 59 you will have a better sense of your income in retirement. That said, if you do know beyond a shadow of a doubt that you'll always be able to afford the premiums and if you are afraid that if you wait, you may suffer an illness that would make you ineligible for long-term care insurance, then it's fine to go ahead and buy long-term care insurance in your early 50s.

Second, let's look at cost. Let's say that instead of buying a policy now at $2,300 a year, you invested that amount of money for nine years in a Treasury Bond Fund, and that you averaged just 4 percent a year on those funds. In nine years you would have $23,514. Now let's look at what a premium for the same policy would be at age 59 assuming you were in the same state of health: $3,382 a year, assuming there are no price increases (a big assumption). That is a difference of about $1,082 a year in what insurance would cost you at age 50. If you took that $25,314 and just left it in that Treasury Bond fund, it would generate about $1,013 a year in interest.

That is pretty close to the $1,082 dollars more a year you would need. Moreover, you've been accumulating assets rather than paying premiums during those nine years.

There are risks to this strategy. One is that something might happen to you during those nine years that would call for long-term care insurance. Only you can determine the size of that risk and your tolerance for it. Another is that premiums will go up for new policy holders but not for those who are currently owners of a policy. Finally, you should take into consideration that you will have lost nine years of the compounding of your daily benefit amount. So if you bought a policy at age 50 for $130 a day benefit with an inflation rider of 5 percent compounding, then when you were 59 your benefit amount would have grown to be worth $202. To be even, you might want to buy a policy in which the benefit starts at $202 a day when you are 59.

I repeat, however, that my biggest reason for advising you to wait until 59 is to make sure you have a grip on your long-term financial picture so that you know you can truly afford your policy until the day that you use it or die.

I'm 68 years old. Have I missed the boat?

It depends on your financial situation. Your premiums are going to be a lot higher than if you had bought earlier, but the cost could still be well worth it, if you can afford to pay it. Say your policy costs you about $3,000 a year, more than twice as much as if you had purchased it in your 50s. If you enter a nursing home at age 84, you will have paid $3,000 a year for 16 years, or $48,000. That's a lot of money, but what if you are in that nursing home for one year (a year and nine months less than the average stay)? Sixteen years from now it will cost well over $100,000 a year to live in a pleasant nursing home, more than twice what you will have paid in premiums. I realize this example does not take into consideration what would happen if you had invested the premiums instead of buying a policy, but the point is still valid, for most people do not invest their premiums annually. Almost everyone over the age of 49 is a good candidate for long-term care insurance. I don't care how high your premium will be, the total cost of your long-term care policy is most likely going to be less than the cost of one year in a nursing home. So even at age 68, long-term care insurance still makes sense for you, if you can afford it.

How much should long-term care insurance cost me?
You should spend no more than 5 to 7 percent of your monthly income on premiums. This is a type of insurance where it really pays to compare prices because policies vary significantly in terms of the benefits they offer.

That said, you may not have to pay as much as you think you will if you find the right company. Based on your age and assuming that you are in excellent health, below is one example of what an excellent long-term care policy with a $167 daily benefit amount, six-year coverage, 30-day elimination period, lifetime benefits, a compound 5 percent inflation provision, and full nursing-home and home-care coverage might cost you in 2006. (I'll explain more about the benefits you should look for below.)

ANNUAL PREMIUMS

AGE	COST
54	$2,615
55	$2,720
56	$2,856
57	$3,021
58	$3,201

AGE	COST
59	$3,382
60	$3,637
61	$3,878
62	$4,148
63	$4,419
64	$4,704
65	$5,005
66	$5,351
67	$5,741
68	$6,268
69	$6,839
70	$7,485

Please note: The daily benefit amount, the benefit period, the elimination period, the inflation provision, and the home health-care coverage will all need to be identical when comparing prices among different companies. There can be big pricing differences among companies offering long-term care insurance (or any insurance, for that matter). I have seen policies from two or three carriers offering essentially the same benefits with a difference of up to $1,500 a year. When you compare prices, make sure that you are comparing apples with apples—comparing policies with exactly the same benefits across the board. Otherwise your price comparisons won't yield the information you're really looking for.

What should I look for in a long-term care policy?

You should look for an appropriate daily benefit amount that reflects the cost of skilled-facility care in your area, an adequate benefit period, an elimination period that's between zero and 50 days, an inflation provision, and home health-care coverage.

What is the daily benefit amount?

The *daily benefit amount* tells you the maximum amount the policy will pay per day if you use the benefits. Policies are now being sold in two ways: the original way, in which there is a specific fixed amount of money that the policy will pay per day for your nursing-home stay or your home health care, and a *pool-of-money* design or benefit account. Policies generally offer between $50 and $400 a day for nursing care and 50 to 100 percent of nursing-care benefit levels for home healthcare. If the policy that you are considering is sold under the original guidelines, as of the year 2007 I would recommend purchasing about a $167-a-day benefit (without considering the inflation provision, which I'll say more about later), which is the average cost of nursing care today. Ultimately, the benefit amount you select will depend on how much of your care you expect the policy to pay for. Calculate the daily benefit amount you need by estimating how much other income you will have and will be willing to apply to a long-term care stay at the time you might need to begin using benefits.

Traditional policies that offer a daily benefit amount work in tandem with the *benefit period.* For example, if you bought a four-year policy that offered a $100-a-day benefit amount, you would have a policy that would pay up to $100 a day for four years in a facility or at home.

These days, however, more and more policies are being offered with a better way of calculating benefits, in my opinion—based on what is known as a pool-of-money or benefit-account approach. In the pool-of-money or benefit-account design, the policy starts off looking like the traditional policies, in which you purchase a specific benefit amount for a specific period of time. However, in the new policies, the insurer takes the total amount of benefits you have purchased with your premiums and conceptually puts it in a benefit account. At claim time, that account can be accessed for any kind of covered service. Using the example of a four-year plan at $100 a day, this would mean that the insured has $146,000 (without considering inflation benefits) available to fund his or her care needs within the daily or monthly policy limits. This results in a policy that will pay for home health care or a nursing home, in any order, in any combination, for as long as the pool of money or benefit account lasts. So, even though the original policy that was purchased this way had a four-year benefit period, in reality there is no four-year limit on your use of the policy; the only real limit is the $146,000 ceiling that was established when the policy was purchased. When the pool of funds or benefit account runs out, your coverage ends. This is a good way to use your coverage to best meet your needs.

What is a benefit period?

The *benefit period* is the length of time some of the older policies will pay for your long-term care. For an individual, I recommend choosing a four- to six-year plan; for qualifying couples, I recommend choosing a six- to eight-year shared plan, if your insurance company offers it.

What is an elimination period?

It's like the deductible in your medical insurance. It is the time period during your initial stay in a nursing home, to take one type of long-term care option, when you will not receive benefits. Such periods are typically between zero and 100 days, and you are responsible for paying your costs until the period ends. Compare the premium costs between a shorter elimination period (say, zero to 30 days) and a longer period (60 to 90 days). If the difference in premium cost is not significant (it will usually be just $100 to $200 a year), consider buying the shortest possible elimination period you can afford in order to adequately protect your assets and estate. If it is available and you can afford it, I always recommend a zero-day elimination period, but your elimination period should never be longer than 50 days. Think about it—wouldn't you rather pay an extra $200 a year now versus your expenses of about $300 a day, years from now, for 30 to 90 days? If it pains you to pay less than a dollar a day for that extra coverage today, how are you going to feel about payments of about $300 a day down the road? Be smart and go for the shorter elimination periods.

What is an inflation option provision?

This provision allows for your daily benefit and your lifetime benefit account maximum to increase by a certain percent each year to help keep pace with rising long-term care costs. Some policies may cap this growth by an amount or by an age limitation. Other policies let you increase your benefit maximum every few years by purchasing additional insurance at your current age rate. This is crucial. The younger you are when you purchase your insurance, the more time you will have for the benefit maximum to grow. If you are between the ages of 40 and 70, the best choice will be the 5 percent compound inflation benefit with no age limit or financial cap, if you can afford it. After age 70, the decision to buy an inflation option depends on your particular situation. The 5 percent simple interest choice is less expensive in the early years, but a larger initial benefit may prove to be shortsighted.

What are non-forfeiture benefits?

If you decide to drop your long-term care coverage, non-forfeiture benefits could give you back some of the premiums you've paid in. Sounds good, but please keep in mind that a non-forfeiture benefit can make your premiums up to 35 percent more expensive. If you can afford this, it's probably better to take the extra money and invest it for growth on your own.

What should I look for in the home-health-care provision of a policy?

In general, long-term care means nursing-home care, which means treating a condition from which one is not expected to recover. Home health care (HHC) may include long-term care, but more typically it means care that is provided for shorter periods while one recovers from an accident or illness at home. The home-health-care (HHC) clause allows you to receive certain kinds of care at home if this care is administered by professionals, friends, or individuals deemed qualified by the insurance company. Some plans state that if you belong in a nursing home but would rather be at home instead, the policy will pay your long-term care benefits at home, just as if you were at a nursing home. I view HHC as coverage you would need at home for the short term—for a broken hip, for example. With HHC, you are expected to get well. With long-term care, you are not expected to get better.

As of 2004, many carriers include far more than traditional home care in their policies. There are policies that offer benefits for assisted-living centers, adult day-care centers, adult congregate-living facilities, and other community-based care providers. So it is important that you find a policy that has a broad emphasis on home-care benefits. Make sure to find out what is covered.

Why is it important that an HHC policy offer so many different kinds of care alternatives?

It is important that you have a choice of the kind of care you may want instead of having to take the kind of care that your carrier is willing to pay for. Given that most of us would prefer to avoid being put in a home or being institutionalized at all, it is crucial to know that there are policies out there today that contain options that include being able to move into a private residence that has been converted to allow barrier-free access and has some monitoring staff available around the clock, but that offers you a private room, furnished with your own belongings. This kind of benefit is a growth market for the future. Nursing homes are now mostly providing skilled care for patients who used to be in hospitals. More and more custodial patients are finding better care options outside the nursing home.

Given that the trend is moving toward care outside a nursing home, is it better to purchase an exact daily benefit amount policy or a pool-of-funds reimbursement policy?

Given the situation today, I would lean toward the pool-of-funds or benefit-account design, in which, in the best contracts, you are covered without much regard to site of care. These policies offer an increasing freedom to choose the care you need with a degree of independence.

That said, one thing you need to keep in mind when looking for a good, flexible HHC provision is that the best policies today recognize that true home care is typically not delivered every day. Care is intermittent and relies on an informal caregiver being in place. In the old design, the HHC side of the contract imposed a daily limit, with emphasis on the word *daily*. But what often happens in real life is that the insured receives visits from an aide three times a week and, say, from an RN once a week; under the old rules, if these visits occurred on the same day, the insured might exceed the daily limit and incur out-of-pocket costs. Today's better plans recognize this and treat HHC benefits with a weekly or even a monthly maximum. So if we once again use the example of the policy with a $100-a-day benefit amount but use the pool-of-funds approach, that $100-per-day benefit will automatically have a $700-per-week or $3,100-per-month limit for HHC, allowing for more complete coverage, even on days when multiple services are received.

How much coverage will I need in the home health-care portion of my policy?

In years past, when there were not many options available, I used to recommend 50 percent of the nursing-home long-term care benefit amount for HHC. So if your long-term care daily benefit amount were $100, the HHC daily benefit amount would be $50. I now recommend that your HHC benefit be 100 percent of what the long-term care benefit amount is for three reasons:

1. In major metropolitan areas, HHC services may cost every bit as much as nursing homes do.
2. Although HHC services typically cost less than nursing homes do today, I expect demand will drive up the costs of services in the future.
3. If you purchase the pool-of-funds policy, there is no penalty if the costs of your HHC are much lower, because the money stays in the pool and is available for you to spend on other types of care or on extending the time the current care plan will be active. (To go back to the $146,000 example, it would take eight years to exhaust this benefit if your expenses were only $50 per day, even if you had purchased a four-year plan.)

My husband is in an assisted-living facility. Would LTC insurance have covered this cost?

It depends. Most policies cover care in an assisted-living facility at some level. The definition of a long-term care facility may vary by policy, by insurance company, and by state. Again, you want a policy that is flexible about where you receive care and allows you to have as many options as possible when you need them. But while you want the policy to be flexible, you don't want it to be vague: Ideally, your policy should specify a number of different types of facilities that would be acceptable to you, and it should cover you in all states, in case you move. A good policy will follow you wherever you go in the United States. Make sure it does before you buy it.

What is a waiver of premium?

This means that once you actually begin to receive benefits and continue to receive them, you won't pay premiums. Check to see if there is a stated period of time for you to be receiving benefits before this waiver goes into effect. All good policies should have a waiver. Also, in a good shared policy, once you have been paying premiums for at least ten years *and* one of you begins to need long-term care, premiums should stop for both of you. At the death of the partner needing long-term care, the surviving partner should have a paid-up policy without needing to pay further premiums.

What does restoration of benefits mean?

Let's say you had a four-year benefit period but were able to leave the LTC facility after three years. If you then stay out of the facility for 180 days or more, this provision compels the company to restore your benefits back to the full four years. This way, if you end up in the nursing home again, you will be covered for another four full years. In an individual policy, I would not pay more for this provision. But in a shared policy, if the increase in cost is 6 percent or less of the annual premium *and* the surviving partner's benefit is restored in full after the death of the partner in the nursing home, I would seriously consider it.

My company offers a group long-term care insurance plan. Should I just sign up for that?

Employer-offered group plans may be cheaper than individual plans, but most have longer elimination periods, limited benefit periods, fairly rigid benefits, poor inflation protection, and no spousal discounts. And, depending on the state, they may not be guaranteed renewable. Indeed, your employer and/or the insurance company can cancel the plan without your consent. So check out the costs and benefits of an individual plan and compare them to the plan your employer is offering. Also, if you purchase a group plan, make sure that you can convert your policy into an individual policy should you leave the group, for example, quit your job.

What conditions must be met before the benefits start coming?

Partly, the answer depends on whether your policy is tax-qualified or non-tax-qualified. (Please see page 43 for a complete description of the differences.) Among other differences, tax-qualified and non-tax-qualified policies have different benefit eligibility triggers and definitions for activities of daily living (ADLs), the six activities you need to be able to do to function normally, including bathing, eating, dressing, transferring, continence, and going to the toilet. Typically, your benefits become available to you when you cannot perform two or more of these ADLs, so it's important to ask how each of these is defined in your policy.

Is there anything else I need to look out for when buying a long-term care policy?

Remember that you must be relatively healthy at the time you purchase long-term care insurance. Most policies no longer require it, but check to make sure that a hospital stay is not required before the insurance company will pay for your long-term care in any facility. Your benefits should be as comprehensive as possible: They should cover custodial (or personal) and intermediate care, at home or in an institution, including adult day care.

What else should I look for?

Your benefits should not exclude preexisting conditions, at least not for more than six months after the policy goes into effect. Once you begin receiving benefits, you should not have to pay premiums after a maximum time period of 90 days, including the elimination period, until you are on your own again. You should have to satisfy the elimination period only once, no matter how many times you need care. There should not be any changes in premium levels unless there is an across-the-board increase for everyone who carries the plan in your state, region, or country. It should be a guaranteed renewable plan and have a grace period, keeping your policy in effect in case you forget to make a payment. If you purchase a benefit period that is less than lifetime, make sure that the policy has the "restoration of benefits" feature.

How can I know whether the company I'm thinking about is a good one?

The most important thing to be sure of is that the company you're considering is a financially strong one that is going to remain in the long-term care business over the long haul. When I first started researching long-term care insurance in

1986, there were only about four companies selling it. Today, there are about 130. That number fluctuates at any given time by 30 or 40, depending on which companies have decided to give it a try and which have decided to check out of the long-term care business. Here are the questions you must ask about each company you are considering in order to find out whether the company will still be supplying long-term care benefits when you may need them.

- How long has the company been selling long-term care insurance? The only acceptable answer is ten years, minimum. If the answer is one year, two years, or three years, the company is still experimenting.
- How much LTC insurance does the company currently have in force? The only acceptable answer is hundreds of millions of annual premium dollars. With that much money in long-term care, the company is already making a handsome profit—and not thinking of getting out of the business.
- How many times has the company had a rate increase for those who already own a policy? The only accept able answer is two times or fewer.
- In how many states is the company currently selling long-term care insurance? The only acceptable answer is in every state. Because each state regulates its own insurance policies, and because it is tedious and expensive for insurance companies to be licensed to sell every kind of insurance in every state, if the company is selling long-term care insurance in only one state—yours—you can be sure it is still experimenting.
- Is your company on the block to be sold? The answer you want to hear is no. Even if the company has a great long-term care insurance track record now, what would

happen if the company that bought it wasn't one you felt safe with? A few years ago, for example, American Express, whose insurers had a good policy, decided to sell its long-term care business. It was sold to GE Capital in the end. So prospective American Express long-term care insurance buyers should have been more interested in GE Capital than in American Express. (Happy ending: GE Capital insurers are still committed to long-term care.) So one has to watch it carefully.

- What are the company's ratings from the following independent companies, all of which rate the safety and soundness of insurance carriers?

  AM Best, (908) 439-2200, *www.ambest.com* A+ or better

  Moody's (212) 553-0377, *www.moodys.com* AA or better

  Standard & Poor's (212) 208-8000, *www.standardandpoors.com* AA or better

  Duff & Phelps (312) 263-2610, *www.dufflic.com* AA

  The only acceptable answer is that at least two of the major insurance rating companies must have awarded top ratings to the company you're considering. Insist that the insurance company send you the ratings in writing, or call the ratings companies yourself.

- Is the company certified by the Insurance Marketplace Standard Association (IMSA)? The only acceptable answer is yes. Good companies regulate themselves and their market practices to be able to display this seal of approval.

Life Insurance

Originally, life insurance was designed to protect people while they were relatively young, in case the family breadwinner died early. Later, if the breadwinner survived until the children had grown up and he or she had built a retirement nest egg, the insurance would be canceled.

Today, things are different. A huge industry exists to sell you as much life insurance as it can, whether you need it or not.

I know how the industry works, because I'm a licensed insurance agent as well as a financial planner, and even though selling life insurance is not my favorite thing, I know most policies inside and out. I also know how insurance commissions work. If you had any idea how large those commissions really are—often 80 to 90 percent of the first year's premium—you would know why people say that life insurance isn't something you buy; it's something that's sold to you.

Many people think of life insurance as a universal financial-planning tool, as a safe haven for savings and a substantial legacy for the family after they are gone. As we grow older, however, there are often better places to hold—and grow—our money, and there can be serious disadvantages to leaving a large life insurance policy among our assets when we die. In any case, no one should ever use life insurance, or any kind of insurance, as a savings vehicle.

If you're single and have no dependents at all, you can skip this section, because there is no need for you to have life insurance. However, if you have relatives who depend on the money you bring in with every paycheck, the following information is essential for you to understand.

These are the four basic questions to ask yourself about life insurance:

- Do I need it?
- How much do I need?
- How long will I need it?
- What kind of life insurance policy do I need?

How do I know if I need life insurance?

Here's how. Compile a list of all your family's expenses and total them. After you have done this, review your expenses and figure out how dramatically your family's financial situation would change if your children were suddenly without one or both parents. Fixed expenses, such as the mortgage payment, would remain the same. Some expenses, such as the grocery bill, would decrease. What if the remaining partner had to go to work? Would your child-care situation change? Could the remaining partner's income cover the financial goals you've set for the future—paying for your children's education, for example? How much would it take to live? How much do you have saved?

Now compare the reduced income after the death of one or both parents with the expenses of maintaining the household. If the survivors would have enough to live, then you do not need insurance. You may still want some for peace of mind, but you don't *need* it—and there is a big difference between *needing* insurance and *wanting* it.

If your survivors would not have enough, then you need insurance to protect you and your loved ones.

How much life insurance do I need?

Most people think all they'd need is enough to help their family get by until the members come to terms with the loss. As a result, they usually sign up for the $50,000 or so worth of insurance that's part of their benefits package at work. But since an unexpected death affects different people in different ways, how much insurance you buy is a decision that must be discussed with the people who would be affected. All the questions must be asked: Would they feel comfortable knowing that they have enough money to get by for a year, or two, or eight?

My insurance agent says I don't need to go through all this—that I can just buy enough coverage to replace my salary for eight years. Is that wrong?

Many experts will tell you to purchase six to eight times your annual salary, but experts are not the ones who have to live your dependents' lives. You might prefer to know that everyone will be OK no matter what, even if no one is ever able to work again. Perhaps you want to provide for your children for ten years, rather than eight. Each of us has our own financial what-if comfort level. The final decision should strike a balance between security and affordability.

Is there any kind of financial guideline you can give me?

An ideal death benefit would be equal to twenty times your beneficiaries' income needs. I know that sounds like a lot, but if your policy is that large your survivors will be able to invest the proceeds in safe bonds (yielding 5 percent) and live off the income without having to dip into the principal. That's a tremendous amount of security for them. And if you stick with term insurance, I think you will be surprised at how affordable a large policy can be.

What's the theory behind that recommendation?
This is the idea: You want your insurance payment to be a sum of money that your beneficiaries can invest to generate enough income to cover their expenses without having to dip into the principal. If they end up having to use up some of the principal each year to meet their living expenses, they will eventually run out of money. You don't want that to happen.

In my case, if I die, I know that my wife would need to have some support, but she makes the same amount of money I do and I know she would continue to work. How do I figure out what she would need?
Assuming you also have monthly expenses of $3,000, in theory, all she would need from the insurance proceeds before taxes is $1,500 a month. (That is, assuming her financial needs will be roughly equal to what they were for both of you when you were still alive.) You have three choices. You can purchase the minimum amount of insurance needed to cover that shortage of $1,500 a month, which is $360,000 worth, plus whatever will be needed for first-year expenses (about $18,000). Or you can purchase $720,000 worth of insurance to cover all your expenses in case, at some later date, your wife won't be able to work. Or you can purchase any amount in between that would make you both feel comfortable.

OK, let's say that my wife needs only $1,500 a month. But I've bought a $720,000 policy, so investing half of that—actually, at 5 percent interest, a little more than half—should cover her needs. What should she do with the remainder of the $720,000?
She will want to invest enough safely for the principal to generate that $1,500 a month every year, without touching the

principal. The rest she should invest for growth in case the day comes when she loses her job. If you had decided simply to purchase the minimum amount of insurance needed in this situation, which was $360,000, she would have to invest all of that to generate the $1,500 a month income she needed and hope she was able to keep on working while she built up a nest egg.

I did everything you said and I talked to my insurance agent, and the bottom line is, we just can't afford to buy as much insurance as I would like. Any suggestions?
Make sure your agent is pricing term life insurance for you. Term is far less expensive than other forms of life insurance that go by names such as whole life, universal life, and variable life. I strongly believe that term is the best insurance for the vast majority of people, and it literally costs a fraction of the other forms of life insurance. Insurance agents who rely on commissions are not necessarily going to recommend the least expensive option to you. But I will: term life insurance is an affordable way to protect your family.

Are there any quote services that you particularly recommend?
Yes. Check with at least three of the following services; you would be surprised how much they can differ.

Select Quote: (800) 343-1985; *www.selectquote.com*
Accuquote: (800) 442-9899; *www.accuquote.com*
Insurance Quote Services: (800) 972-1104;
www.iquote.com
Term-quote: (800) 444-8376; *www.termquote.com*
Master Quote of America: (800) 337-5433;
www.masterquote.com

Liferates: (800) 457-2837; *www.liferates.com*
Insure.com: (800) 431-1147; *www.insure.com*

How long will I need to keep my life insurance policy?
That depends. As the years go by, the money that you're saving in your retirement plans, the money you accumulate on your own, and the mortgage you're paying toward owning your house outright will change how much insurance you need, or whether you need it at all. One of your goals should be to make sure that by the time you are retired, you'll have enough income from your retirement plans to support yourself and, later, your loved ones after you're gone. Once you have enough to live on, there will probably be no need for life insurance. That said, never, *never* cancel or attempt to change a policy without checking with your doctor and having a thorough physical, as you may want to keep insurance you otherwise would not have needed for medical reasons. Bottom-line goal: By the time you are 65, at the latest, your need for life insurance, and your need to pay the premiums on your life insurance, should be gone.

What kind of life insurance do I need?
In my opinion, there is only one kind of life insurance that makes sense for the vast majority of us: term life insurance. When you sign up for term insurance, you're buying a just-in-case policy for a finite length of time. These policies are not very expensive, especially if you're fairly young, because the insurance company knows you have relatively little chance of dying while the policy is in force.

I am 25 years old and single with no dependents. Should I buy life insurance?
In this situation, you probably don't need life insurance as

much as you need to be saving for your retirement and possibly increasing your disability coverage. On the other hand, the younger you are, the cheaper your life insurance premiums will be, which is useful if you purchase a 20- or 30-year term policy with your future spouse and children in mind.

What is the difference between term life insurance and a cash value policy, also known as whole life insurance? Term life insurance protects you for a certain number of years (typically 1 to 20), and once the "term" of the policy is over, you can usually renew the policy and begin another term without providing evidence of your insurability, though often at a higher cost. If you die during the term of the policy, the insurance company pays out a specific amount of money (called the death benefit) to your beneficiaries. Because you do not build any cash value and are paying for protection for a specific length of time, it follows that when you are younger, term life insurance is the least expensive kind of life insurance. However, the older you get, the more expensive term insurance becomes, since it is more likely that the company will have to pay out the death benefit. By the time you are in your 70s, the premiums on term life insurance will be very high but, if you have planned properly, you should no longer need it.

A cash value policy, or what is more commonly known as a whole life policy, is a "permanent" policy, in which you are guaranteed coverage for life. Your premiums are priced accordingly, since the insurance companies know that, unless you let the policy lapse, they will sooner or later have to pay out the death benefit. These policies have a cash value, which means that the insurance company takes your annual premium, deducts some administrative fees and a profit margin plus the cost of death protection, and puts the rest (your "cash value") into a savings account.

Which is better: term or whole life insurance?

Term life insurance is the most cost-effective insurance you can buy. There is really no comparison. Term life insurance policies are cheap. Why? Because people are living longer—beyond the term of coverage—so insurance companies don't have to pay out as many life insurance claims. This is key to understanding life insurance: Insurance companies sell insurance to make money. They will sell you a term policy at a reasonable rate when you are young because they know it is unlikely that you are going to die during the term. You want a flexible policy that offers you security without costing very much, because you probably won't ever need to use it. Whole life insurance is mostly just a costly way to maintain a savings account.

Are there different types of term life insurance policies?

Yes. You can buy what is known as a "level" term policy. With a level term policy, your premiums would be level for the term you have chosen, usually 5, 10, 15, or 20 years. The insurance company takes your current age and the term you choose into consideration and figures out the average stable premium you will have to pay to keep the policy in effect for all those years. Obviously, the older you are and the longer the term you sign up for, the higher the premium will be.

You can also buy annual guaranteed-renewable term insurance, where, at the end of each year if you renew the policy, the premiums increase to reflect your new age.

Another option is decreasing term insurance (which is normally used by people whose main financial obligation also decreases, like a mortgage). This kind of policy starts with a specific death benefit that decreases each year until your policy expires at zero.

The last kind of term insurance is not as commonly needed or sold, but you may come across it: increasing term life insurance, which provides a death benefit that rises steadily as the term continues.

If I get term life insurance, what size term should I look for?

The longest period of coverage that you can purchase is usually no more than 30 years. Many people, not only salespeople, may tell you to buy the longest term you can in order to lock in a relatively low rate. However, I recommend buying a term long enough for you to save the money to take care of your family on your own, through your own investments and savings.

My insurance agent offers policies that have names other than whole and term. Are there different types of cash value accounts?

Yes. The most common types are whole life, universal life, and variable life. Whole life and universal life policies mean that the insurance company will invest your cash value and give you a declared (though variable) interest rate. Variable life policies give you mutual-fund type options for your cash value and you can choose how to invest those funds.

So does my death benefit grow as my cash value accumulates?

In most cases, no. This is a decision you make when you purchase this type of insurance. Your death benefit is constant, which means it is paid out at the same rate at any time for as long as the policy is in effect. Your premiums are also constant in cash value policies, and are designed to remain the same until the policy matures at an age set by your particular policy, usually 95 or 100 (the age when your premium payments would cease and the cash value would equal the face amount). Most people, obviously, do not expect to live to age 100.

My insurance agent told me that cash value life insurance is better because it offers tax-favored growth. Is that true?

Yes and no. Money that you invest in a cash value life insurance policy will grow tax-deferred—if and when it grows. It is not uncommon for a whole life policy to lose money in its first five or six years, in part because of the commissions and administrative fees. Remember, the commissions on most cash value policies are high. This may explain why your insurance agent is so enthusiastic about this type of policy. There are many other ways to invest and reduce taxes without paying a commission or lots of fees: Put your money in an IRA or a 401(k) and you'll find a similar tax benefit and, the odds are, more growth.

What is universal life insurance?

This is a variation of whole life insurance, except that the investment portion of your insurance premiums goes into money-market funds and grows at a variable rate. After your first payment, this type of policy allows you to pay premiums at any time and in any amount within a particular minimum and maximum rate set in the contract. The premiums you pay and the interest that your money earns is the amount of cash value that your policy has at any given time, less the expenses of the insurance company, which can be considerable and can also increase over time. As with whole life insurance, the insurance company makes many of the investment decisions.

Because whole life and universal policies have cash values, if you decide not to keep your policy, or if you suddenly need money while you're alive, you can cash out. But commissions on life insurance policies are some of the most lucrative commissions in any business—and once you've paid them, you can't get them back. If your goal in buying life insurance is to put money aside, there are far, far better ways to save.

What is variable life insurance?

Similar to whole life insurance, this type of policy provides death benefits or cash values that vary according to the investment returns of stock and bond funds managed by your insurance company (although you can choose where to invest your premiums). This can be a very uncertain type of policy because your premiums change and there is no guaranteed cash value, although theoretically it can pay off at higher rates than whole or universal life policies. Remember, though, that the risk is to your money.

Can I borrow money against a whole life insurance policy?

You can take out what is called a policy loan, as long as it doesn't exceed the cash value your policy will have on its next anniversary. In many cases, you don't ever have to repay this loan, since the amount of money left in the policy generates enough interest to pay the loan charges. If you don't repay the loan, however, your death benefit decreases by the amount of your loan plus interest. The interest rate you have to pay for a loan is set in your contract.

I realize that you don't recommend it but, if I wanted to, could I convert a term policy into a whole life policy?

Yes, many term policies are "convertible," which means they can be exchanged for another type of policy, including whole life. Frequently, this involves paying the difference between the premiums for the two policies. But in most cases, I'd advise you not to do this. If you are unhappy with your term insurance for some reason, look for a different term policy that will better meet your needs. Make sure your new policy is in force before you drop your old one.

OK, I made the big mistake and bought a whole life policy. What should I do with it now?

First, you need to go to a doctor and make sure that you have a clean bill of health. Then you can apply for and purchase a term life insurance policy for whatever length of time you think you require in order to save enough money to provide for your family if you die. Once you have been approved for your new term policy, then and only then should you cash out your whole life policy and invest the "cash value" in a good no-load mutual fund. Add to your investment what you're saving on premiums, which will be much lower now.

I told my insurance agent that I want to cash out my whole life policy but he says I'm crazy because it's only over the long run that these policies make money. He says if I take it out now I'll be losing money. Is that true?

You may be losing some of your investment in the short term because the insurance company has deducted so many fees, but you are almost certainly going to make it up and then some over the long run (ten or more years) if you invest that cash value and the excess premium money in a no-load mutual fund. The insurance company is the party that is really going to lose money, because they won't have the use of yours anymore.

Will I have to pay taxes if I cash my whole life insurance policy out?

If you cancel the policy, you get a lump sum payout and you will pay taxes on it only if the cash value plus your dividends equals more than the total of all the premiums that you paid into it—frequently, it won't be, which is why you are cashing it out in the first place.

What happens if I stop paying my premiums on a whole life insurance policy?

Usually you have a certain amount of time (often a few years) to reinstate or renew the policy, as long as you can establish your insurability again. If you find yourself in this situation, don't just automatically get your old policy reinstated. Make sure that it is still better than any new policy you could get.

What is double indemnity?

Many life insurance policies pay double the death benefit if the death of the insured is accidental. For instance, if your death happened because of a car accident, and you had this feature on a $200,000 policy, it would pay out at $400,000. Medical emergencies, such as heart attacks, do not count. It should be noted, however, that this benefit is paid very infrequently. For example, if the insured gets into an accident and dies after 90 days, most policies with this feature will not pay the double indemnity benefit. This benefit is largely a scare tactic, and not worth the cost.

Is suicide covered in a life insurance contract?

If the policy doesn't specifically exclude it, suicide often becomes covered two years after you purchase your policy. During those two years, if the insured commits suicide, the insurance company normally returns the premiums but doesn't pay out a death benefit.

My husband of ten years just died. When I notified his life insurance company, I found out that his first wife is still the beneficiary on his policy! They didn't even speak to one another and I know he must not have realized that he never made the switch. Is there any way to challenge this?

Unfortunately, it will be difficult and expensive to challenge your husband's mistake. You will have to notify the insurance company of your intent to dispute the beneficiary, and it will be up to a court to decide whether your claim is appropriate, which often requires proving that your spouse was incompetent. This is why it is crucial that you review your insurance policies periodically and make sure that everything is up to date.

I've just had a baby. Now my mom is telling me that I will need to buy life insurance in my newborn daughter's name. Is this a good idea?

No, don't do it. Remember, life insurance is meant to replace income that other people are dependent on. Your baby has no income and doesn't need her own life insurance. She needs your life insurance, if something should happen to you.

Is it ever a good idea to take out a life insurance policy on another person?

It can be, if you have a financial interest in that person, usually a spouse or a business partner.

Do you always need to take a medical exam before you can buy life insurance?

Almost always. The major exception is if your employer offers life insurance through a group policy.

If I have a terminal illness, is it too late for me to get life insurance?

In most cases, yes. Major insurers will generally not sell you life insurance under these circumstances, although certain people with HIV may be able to purchase such a policy.

What is a living death benefit?

These are riders on life insurance policies, also known as accelerated death benefits. They pay out your death benefit while you are still alive, usually if a doctor certifies that you are terminally ill with less than a year to live. The idea is that you can use these funds for medical care or comfort. The benefit may increase the price of your premiums and usually doesn't pay as much as your heirs would have received after your death.

What is a viatical settlement?

This is another expensive option used almost exclusively by people who are terminally ill. A viatical company will pay you part of the cash value of your whole life insurance policy while you are still alive in exchange for ownership of your policy. They will continue to pay your premiums and they will collect the full benefit after you die. This is a good option if you really need the cash, but it means that you are selling your policy for less than it is worth. It also means you are not leaving your death benefit to the loved ones whom you purchased the policy to protect.

My brother and his wife got a second-to-die life insurance policy. What is that?

This type of insurance, which is sometimes called a survivorship life policy, insures two people, usually spouses, and doesn't pay until both insured people have died. Such a policy is normally worth considering only if you are going to leave a very large estate that will incur substantial estate taxes.

Federal tax law allows you to leave an unlimited amount of money, tax-free, to your spouse. When your spouse dies, the federal taxes will be due on both your estates, and usually must be paid within nine months of the death of the second spouse. A second-to-die life insurance policy could theoretically be used to cover those taxes.

Keep in mind that, as of 2007, federal estate taxes are due only when your estate is worth more than $2 million (anything over the exempt amount will be taxed at a rate of 45 percent). The exempt amount increases in 2009 to $3.5 million, and unless Congress votes to change the law, the estate tax is scheduled to be repealed for 2010 and revert to $1 million in 2011. If you don't have this amount of wealth, don't even think about buying such a policy. If you think that your estate will be large enough to be subject to federal estate taxes, see a good estate-planning lawyer before you buy one. You may be able to avoid estate taxes in ways that make more financial sense for you, such as establishing trusts.

Is there anything else I need to consider when purchasing second-to-die life insurance?

Ask the agent what would happen in the event that you and your spouse divorced. Is there any provision that allows you to divide or alter the policy? Also, find out what provisions the policy makes, if any, should the estate-tax laws change in a way that would make the insurance unnecessary.

Can I make a trust the beneficiary of my life insurance policy?

Yes. Once your trust is set up, just ask your insurance company what specific language is required when you designate the trust as your beneficiary. (You might, for example, need to designate the name of your trustee, in his or her capacity as trustee.)

Is there any other way to reduce the amount of life insurance I need?

If you are married, you can consider joint and survivor benefits from your retirement plan to make sure part of your income will continue to be provided to your spouse. When you retire and are entitled to begin receiving your pension, you will have a series of joint and survivor options, which means that you can choose what percentage of your monthly pension you want your spouse to receive after you die. If you take a reduced payment while you are alive, your spouse will receive proportionally more after you die. This can reduce your life insurance needs.

I'm going to go for the 50 percent joint and survivor benefit for my wife because I figure she'll need about half my income since one can live more cheaply than two. Does that sound right?

That's a very common way of thinking about your joint and survivor benefits, but it is often wrong. Even though your wife will only need to support herself after you die, her cost of living may continue to rise. All her bills aren't going to be cut in half when you die. For example, the taxes on your home, if you own one, will only increase, as will the costs of maintaining the property. Find out how much money would be deducted from your pension check if your joint and survivor benefit was as high as it could be (100 percent) and consider whether you'll really miss the extra money.

Disability Insurance

We are more likely to consider how to take care of our families after we die than we are to consider how we would take care of ourselves, and them, if we were to become disabled. Just think about it—if you were injured so severely that you could no longer work, how would you pay your bills? In financial terms, disability is potentially more problematic than dying. Dead, you have no further expenses. Disabled, you not only can't work but your expenses may be higher, depending on what kind of medical care and services you need to accommodate your disability.

What is disability insurance and who needs it?

If you were seriously ill or injured, disability insurance replaces a portion of the salary you were making before you became disabled and unable to work. Single and self-employed people should seriously consider disability policies if there would not be financial support from another source if you became so sick or injured that you were unable to work. Even if you have a partner who could make up some of your income, you need to consider whether you and your family could survive comfortably without your salary.

How is disability defined?

A disability is defined as a limitation of your physical or mental ability to work resulting from sickness or injury. It may be partial, in which case you are unable to perform certain job functions, or total, in which case you are unable to work at all.

Is disability insurance the same thing as worker's compensation?

No. Worker's compensation protects you if you are injured while performing your job. Disability insurance is a form of health insurance that replaces all or part of your income while you are injured or ill for any reason. You may already have disability coverage if you work for a large company. You normally start receiving disability benefits three to six months after you become injured and unable to work.

Doesn't the Social Security Administration (SSA) insure me if I'm disabled?

It surely does, but there are good reasons for going to the private insurance market for disability insurance, if you can afford it.

What sort of coverage is offered by the SSA?

Not a whole lot. The average disability benefit in the United States (paid out, incidentally, to approximately 6.4 million workers across the country) was $895 a month for 2005. But this benefit can make a huge difference to a disabled worker and his family.

Who qualifies?

It depends on your age and when you become disabled. (See *Ask Suze... About Social Security*.)

The SSA has compiled a list of conditions that it considers "disabling," as follows:

- Heart disease of any kind, or chronic obstructive lung disease (emphysema), conditions which might result in the prolonged and persistent loss of heart or lung strength. These conditions must be confirmed by a test, such as an EKG or an X ray.
- Acquired Immune Deficiency Syndrome (AIDS) and any related diseases, for example, pneumonia.
- Chronic arthritis, which causes pain, inflammation, swelling, and limited movement and mobility.
- Any type of brain disease that causes a diminution of judgment, memory, or intellect.
- Cancer.
- Loss of function in a limb.
- Serious kidney disease of any kind.

- Any diseases of the gastrointestinal system that result in severe physical diminishment.
- Muteness.
- Blindness.
- Deafness, if it presents a seriously impaired ability to get along with other people, such that it prevents gainful employment.

Is it possible to be declared disabled by a commercial insurance company and not by the Social Security Administration?

Yes. Each insurance company sets its own eligibility requirements. It is entirely possible to be deemed disabled by a commercial insurance company and not by the Social Security Administration. A key question often is, Disabled for what sort of work? To receive benefits, the SSA requires that you be disabled from doing almost any sort of work, while commercial companies may require only that you be disabled from doing your own particular line of work. Of course, the cost for broad coverage can be high.

So under SSA rules, I mustn't be able to work at all?

Not "gainful" work. The Social Security Administration defines gainful employment as any employment from which you are earning $900 or more per month.

Can a person survive solely on Social Security disability benefits?

It's extremely difficult, if not impossible. For that reason and others, it is important that you find out whether there is any job that your limited physical condition will permit you to do. It is also important that you find out exactly what benefits you may have coming to you from any other sources. Remember, the Social Security Administration with all its attendant benefits, whether retirement, disability, survivors, or dependents, was initiated in the 1930s as a kind of rock-bottom safety net, not as a replacement for your entire income.

Private Commercial Disability Insurance

I hope I've said enough about the SSA's disability insurance program to indicate its weaknesses—that is, your vulnerabilities if you depend on it. The benefits are by no means to be sneezed at. Nor, for that matter, are the disability insurance plans that may be available through your employer, usually in the form of workmen's compensation. For many people, however, the coverage provided by social insurance of this nature is simply not enough—for them or their families. To find out if they are enough for you, ask yourself a hard question: If I were to become seriously ill or injured, could I and my family survive comfortably without my earned income? If the answer is no, then commercial disability insurance is the way to go.

What should I look for in a disability policy?

Ideally you should have coverage that would pay you the typical maximum benefit of 66 percent of your income after an accident that leaves you unable to work at your current job. It should cover you in case of an illness or an accident, it should always be noncancelable guaranteed renewable, and, in the best case, should offer a residual benefit protection.

Beyond that, I would want a policy that covered me for what is known as "owner's occupation," not "any occupation." As I said, this is the option that most sharply differentiates what's available on the market from what social insurance offers. An owner's-occupation policy means that if I become disabled and can no longer perform my current occupation, regardless of what other kinds of work I might be able to do, the insurance company will pay me benefits. An any-occupation policy would pay me only if I could not perform any job at all. Let's say I'm a writer and for some reason become disabled and unable to write. I would want my disability policy to pay me benefits even though I might be able, for example, to sell fruit from a cart. An any-occupation policy, of course, wouldn't pay unless I were unemployable.

Why is it so crucial that my disability insurance be noncancelable and guaranteed renewable?

Because if it isn't, your insurance company can cancel your policy. This way, the only reason your policy can be canceled is if you stop paying your premiums. Also, your insurance company cannot increase the premium (generally until age 65) or change any policy provisions.

My agent suggested a modified-occupation disability policy. What does that mean?

This policy will pay you benefits only if you can't work at a job considered appropriate for someone of your age, education, and experience. Note that this might not mean the same job you had before. Say you play the violin in your city's orchestra but you have an accident, which seriously injures your hands. A modified-occupation disability policy would probably not pay out as long as you were still able to teach violin classes at a local college, for instance. Ask your agent to give you examples of what types of jobs you would be considered "qualified" for in a variety of different disabling circumstances. If the options would be unacceptable to you, you'll want to make sure that you have owner's-occupation coverage.

What if I can work at a new job, but it doesn't pay as well as the one I had when I became disabled?
This is another case in which it is important to know that you have the right kind of disability policy. You want your policy to have something called residual benefits, which means it will guarantee a certain percentage of your old job's income in comparison to your new job's income. For example, if your policy guarantees you a 66 percent residual benefit and you became disabled, you would be guaranteed 66 percent of the income you made in your old job. So if you were making $80,000 before your accident, but your new, post-accident job pays only $50,000, your insurance company will have to pay you $2,800 each year to make up the difference between your new salary ($50,000) and 66 percent of your old salary ($52,800).

What kind of elimination period should disability insurance have?
The elimination period, which is the amount of time after your injury or the onset of your illness when you receive no benefits, varies from policy to policy. Try not to have more than a 60-day elimination period. In the meantime, make sure that you are working toward establishing an emergency fund for yourself, if you have not already done so, so that you could cover the costs of living for a few months without your pay check.

Would my disability benefits increase over time if I were disabled forever?
This is an important question. You would find it difficult, or impossible, to live on an income that doesn't keep pace with inflation. Cost of living adjustments (COLAs) or riders cover this possibility and they may be included in your policy or they may cost extra. These riders allow you to increase your cover-

age (and your premiums, usually modestly) periodically without having an additional physical.

Car Insurance

Most of us know a little something about car insurance, probably more than we know about our medical insurance. Why? Because we are required by the state we live in to have certain types of coverage. But the state-mandated amount of coverage may not be enough. On the other hand, agents are only too happy to sell us *more* than enough. In this section, I hope to clarify what's the right amount for you.

What are the different kinds of standard coverage I can get for my car?
Standard car insurance includes four types of protection: auto liability, medical payments, collision, and comprehensive coverage.

Auto liability coverage protects you in case you cause an accident. It has two parts. The first is bodily injury liability, which pays your medical expenses and those of anyone else injured in the accident. There is no deductible for this portion of the coverage. Most states require you to have a minimum amount of liability coverage, but bear in mind that the minimum may not be adequate if, for example, you cause a serious accident and get sued for pain and suffering. You can also buy *medical payments* coverage, which will pay your expenses and those of your passengers if you experience a serious injury in a car crash, whether you caused the accident or not. Note, though, that car insurance medical benefits won't pay all medical expenses. There are limits.

The second part of the standard liability policy pays the repair expenses if you accidentally damage somebody else's property (like another person's car or house) with your car.

Collision insurance is an option. It is typically not required by the state. Among other things, it protects your car in the event of an accident, whether you caused the accident or not. If your car is valuable, this might make sense. You can choose whether or not to have a deductible.

Comprehensive insurance, which is also optional, pays for the repair or replacement of your car if it is damaged by a fire, a falling object, an earthquake, a flood, theft, vandalism, or another type of non-automotive accident.

I keep seeing all those numbers that look like dates when I hear about auto liability. What does 30/50/20 mean, for example?

These numbers refer to the limits of your liability policy in a particular accident. If you have these particular numbers, it means you have $30,000 in bodily injury coverage per person, $50,000 in bodily injury coverage per accident, and $20,000 in coverage for property damage.

How much liability coverage should I have?

Standard minimum recommendations for homeowners and people with significant assets are at least $100,000 in bodily injury coverage per person, $300,000 in bodily injury coverage per accident, and $50,000 in property damage liability. Those with fewer assets should consider $15,000 in bodily injury coverage per person, $30,000 in bodily injury coverage per accident, and $10,000 in property damage liability.

Can my whole family and all of my cars be covered by one policy?

Yes, usually, although you don't have to set it up that way. Generally, eligible cars are any four-wheel vehicles owned by an individual or married couple, or leased under contract for at least six months. If one of you has a motorcycle or a motor home, for example, you may have to purchase additional coverage.

Apparently I live in a no-fault state. What does this mean, and do I need liability coverage?

Most states use a no-fault auto insurance system. Other states use traditional third-party systems to settle claims. No-fault states require drivers and their insurance companies to pay their own costs after a car accident, whether they were responsible or not. But you still may need liability insurance, because if you cause an accident and the costs to the other injured people are above a certain threshold, they can sue you. If they win a judgment against you and you don't have sufficient liability coverage, the difference may have to come out of your own pocket. In a state with a traditional third-party system, or a "fault" state, your insurance company pays your claim only if you can prove that you did not cause the accident.

Is the medical payments coverage required?

No-fault states typically require you to buy medical payments coverage, while fault states do not. An argument for buying this type of coverage anyway is that it will pay no matter who caused the accident.

Couldn't my medical insurance pay for this?

Good question: It pays to be on the lookout for duplicate coverage! You're quite right, your medical insurance might cover *you* in such a circumstance. But beware: It won't cover any passengers or other injured parties who are not covered by your health-care policy.

How do I know how much collision and comprehensive coverage I need?

This is generally the more expensive part of car insurance. It is optional in all states, although if you lease your car or take out a loan to buy it, the dealer or bank that loaned you the money will probably require you to purchase it. Most companies have vehicle pricing services. Blue book valuations are not used very much. Most companies will insure for the price you paid for the car, as long as it was a reasonable cost. As usual, if the deductible is higher, you can reduce the price of the premiums.

Should my car insurance reimburse me for my replacement costs or for the actual cash value of my car if it's stolen or damaged?

It will cost you more in premiums to have replacement cost coverage, but it may be worthwhile because such coverage will replace or repair your car without deducting for its depreciation. Actual cash value policies only pay you for the value of the car at the time it is stolen or damaged, which is reduced to account for depreciation.

What if my car is damaged in an accident by a driver with no insurance? Do I have to pay for everything myself?

There is insurance you can purchase, called uninsured-motorists coverage, that would protect you in these circumstances. (There is also uninsured motorist property damage and a collision deductible waiver.) Some states require you to have this coverage; it kicks in if an uninsured driver hits your car and you have medical bills. There is also something called underinsured motorists coverage, which makes up some of the difference if a driver hits you and has some, but not adequate, insurance. In other words, you can make a claim on your own insurance policy if the person who hits you doesn't have any insurance for you to make a claim on. However, note that all of these policies have benefit limits.

How do I know how much car insurance I really need?
The state you live in and, if you borrow money to buy your car, the lending institution, will require you to have certain kinds of coverage. Basic policies usually include some combination of liability, collision, comprehensive, uninsured or underinsured motorist, and medical payments coverage. As for what level of coverage you need, consider your personal situation in order to figure out what will make you feel safe: Is your car brand new or old? How much would it cost you to replace it? Do you have the resources to pay your medical bills and car repairs? Do you have valuable assets you want to protect?

My son just turned 16 and got his driver's license. My car insurance premiums are going to increase like mad if I add him to my policy. Is there anything else I can do?
If your son is going to drive, he's got to have insurance, and insurance companies know that young drivers are risky drivers, so they charge you high rates to protect themselves. If your son isn't going to be taking his car to school every day, you can try to have him classified as an occasional driver, although not all companies will allow you to do this. Many companies do offer modest discounts if he has good grades or has taken a particular type of driver's education course, so ask your agent about these rules. Finally, if you want to save on car insurance costs, not only should you not buy your son a new car, you should have him driving the oldest and cheapest car you own. That is, as long as it's a safe car—saving money on your premiums isn't everything!

Do I have to put my kids on my car insurance policy? Couldn't I make them get their own?
You could, but unless the kids are independently wealthy, you won't save money. In general, it will be more expensive for your teenager to have his own individual car insurance than to increase the premiums on your family policy.

Is there any way to reduce my auto insurance costs?
The premiums on your car insurance are based on, among other things, your age, your sex, where you live, the type of car you drive, and your driving record. However, there are a surprising number of small discounts that it is possible to negotiate. When you price different car insurance policies, make sure the agent knows if you have a clean driving record, because some companies give discounts to drivers who have no points on their licenses. Most insurance companies reduce your premiums based on a combination of your age, sex, and marital status. (Twenty-five is the general rule for single women and married men; 30 is the general rule for single men. Married women are often eligible for the lower rate no matter what their age.) If you are in college or even graduate school and get good grades, some insurance companies will offer you small discounts, even for a few years past graduation. You can check with your company to see how they do it; some demand a GPA of 3.0 or higher, some require you to be on a dean's list, and others want to know that you are in the top 20 percent of your class. Ask your insurance agent for a list of cars that are considered "lower risk" and make sure that your agent knows that your car has air bags and other special safety features, such as an alarm system or antilock brakes, if it does. If there are multiple cars in your house, see if you are entitled to a multiple-car discount.

These discounts might seem arbitrary, but they aren't. All

the discount-qualifying characteristics mentioned above are statistically associated with drivers who have fewer accidents. Umbrella insurance may also reduce your insurance costs.

If my friend drives my car and gets into an accident, will my insurance policy still be effective?
If you loan your car every once in a while, your insurance policy should probably still cover an accident. Rates generally do not increase if a friend is involved in an accident while driving your car.

Homeowner's Insurance

If you financed your home when you purchased it, your lending institution required you to get some insurance on the building. But many people don't have enough coverage, and they pay too much for what they have. Your homeowner's insurance needs to cover the cost of rebuilding or repairing your house if it is damaged in a fire, a storm, a robbery, or other type of catastrophe. Below are the questions and answers that will help you decide if you have the right kind and right amount of insurance for your home.

What should a standard policy for my home cover?
Standard policies generally cover the house and its contents, the latter usually for 50 percent to 70 percent the amount for which you insured the structure. In other words, if you insured your house for $200,000, your policy probably covers the contents of your home up to $100,000 to $140,000. Homeowner's policies also normally include liability coverage for damage or injury incurred inside or outside your house.

What if the contents of my house are worth more than 50 percent of what my home is insured for?

You can increase your content coverage; your premium will increase to cover the additional coverage. Make sure that personal property insurance covers you for the replacement cost of your possessions, not their actual cash value. Figure out how much you need by making a list of everything you own and estimate what it would cost you to replace it all.

What is the difference between an actual cash value policy and a replacement-cost policy?

An actual cash value policy will reimburse you for the cost of your belongings less their depreciation, while a replacement-cost policy means that the insurance company must reimburse you for the actual cost of replacing the lost or damaged item. If you have a couch that you purchased for $1,000 a few years ago, a cash value policy might reimburse you only $800 for that couch, assuming a depreciation of 20 percent, while a replacement-cost policy would pay you enough to get the same couch. You can see why replacement-cost policies are better.

What are the basic types of homeowner's insurance I can buy?

There are six basic types of homeowner's insurance, including renter's and condo owner's coverage.

- HO-1: A basic policy not available in all states. It is rarely purchased by consumers, due to the limited coverage. It covers damage due to falling objects, the weight of ice, snow, or sleet, accidental discharge of water or steam from household appliances, freezing, volcanic eruption, and other perils.

- HO-2: Protects against seventeen perils, including all the perils included in HO-1, plus additional perils of fire, lightning, windstorm, hail, riot, vandalism, and more. People who have mobile homes are normally eligible for a variation of this type of policy.
- HO-3: This is the most common homeowner's policy. It protects your home against all perils except for those that are explicitly excluded by the policy. Some of the excluded perils are earthquakes, floods, termites, landslides, war, tidal waves, and nuclear accidents. Normal wear and tear, mechanical breakdown, vandalism if the home is unoccupied for more than thirty days, and continuous water seepage over a specified period of time are also typical policy exclusions.
- A HO-5 is most often added to HO-3 to expand the coverage to include additional perils.
- HO-4: This is renter's insurance. It does not cover the dwelling or detached structures, which are the landlord's responsibility to insure. It protects the possessions of tenants in a house, apartment, condo, or duplex against the same perils specified in HO-3. It also provides additional living expense, personal liability, and medical payments coverage. Make sure that your policy includes coverage for the replacement cost of your possessions, not their actual cash value.
- HO-6: This is a policy for co-op and condominium owners. Condominium insurance is like HO-4 (renter's) except that it takes into account the fact that you own the inner walls of your condo or town house. It can also fill in any gaps in your condo association's coverage. It is important to note that HO-6 policies include loss assessment coverage; however, the coverage

limit included may be inadequate. If your co-op board or condo association needs to assess charges because of some uninsured loss to the building or liability situation, having substantial loss assessment coverage is important.

- HO-8: This is a type of policy that covers perils like those listed in HO-1, but is meant for people who own older homes. It insures the house only for repair costs or its actual cash value as opposed to its replacement cost in cases when rebuilding the home with the materials and details of the original would be prohibitively expensive. Basically, this policy will pay to restore the damaged property but not at the level of quality or authenticity of the original. This policy is rarely offered.

Each homeowner's policy is divided into two sections. The first part covers your dwelling, other structures on the property, your personal property, and certain types of loss of use, such as rental or additional living expenses. The other part should provide personal liability coverage, medical payments coverage, and additional coverage for claims expenses, first aid, and damage to other people's property.

Why would I need liability coverage in my homeowner's insurance?

This type of coverage is designed to protect your assets if you are sued by someone who is hurt or whose property is damaged due to your negligence. This could be damage you or a member of your family causes or even your pet (although certain types of attack dogs, such as pit bulls and the like, may be excluded from your policy). An example would be if you lived in a two-family house, and you turned the water on to run yourself a bath but then took a phone call. You forgot about your tub, and it overflowed and damaged the ceiling of the unit below you. Liability coverage should pay to repair that damage. You may need special coverage for a home office.

If I already have comprehensive medical coverage, what does the medical payments section cover?

Again, your comprehensive health insurance should pay for you no matter what. This coverage is for protection in the event that *someone else* injures themselves on your property or because of your negligence and needs medical care. The classic example might be your mail carrier falling and injuring his back because your walkway was covered with ice and snow that you failed to remove.

Will homeowner's insurance cover all my personal property?

Regardless of the personal property limit shown on any policy, it is important to know that within this limit for personal property, your policy also contains what are known as "special limits of liability." These are sublimits for special classes of property defined in the policy, such as jewelry, money, silverware, watercraft, business personal property, and such, for which the policy will not pay more than a smaller, set amount. Some of these special class sublimits can be eliminated by the adding of a personal article floater, sometimes known as a rider, to your home, condo, or renter's policy.

I rent one of my extra bedrooms to a college student. Would my homeowner's policy cover her property if my home were broken into?

Usually not, because most policies only cover your property (as the policyholder) and the property of people related to you who live in your house.

So if I have $200,000 in homeowner's insurance and my house is destroyed, do I get $200,000?

Not necessarily. In many policies you actually have to rebuild the structure to get this money, and limits often apply to the cost of rebuilding.

What should I do if something terrible happens and I need to make a claim?

Your insurance company will either send you a "proof of loss" form to complete or will arrange for an adjuster to visit your house. Either way, you need to document your loss as best you can to make sure that you get the full value that you are entitled to under the policy.

Is it true that if I make two homeowner's insurance claims, they can cancel my policy?

It depends on your insurance carrier, but, yes, it can indeed happen. For example, as of 2006, a fairly typical scenario is that you could face nonrenewal if you make more than two claims in a three-year period. So if you can afford it, I always suggest you get a higher deductible and pay for the minor home-related losses out of pocket. Home insurance is for major disasters, not to file small claims so you can get back the money you contributed to premiums. Filing one claim in most cases will do nothing to raise your rates or cancel your policy. But multiple claims, as few as two with certain policies, may cause your insurance company to raise your premiums or even cancel your homeowner's insurance policy. So it is best to get a policy with a high deductible, so that you've got no reason to file lower-cost claims. Another advantage to a higher deductible is that many insurance providers also offer a discount for such a policy.

What is the best way to document my losses?
Make a list of everything that was stolen or damaged, and provide a description of each item, the date you bought it, and, if you have replacement-cost coverage, what it would cost to replace it. If you have receipts, bills, photographs, or serial numbers, these things will generally help your case. Hold onto your damaged items until the adjuster has a chance to look at them. Take photographs or videos of any damage to your house, noting everything you want the adjuster to see, from cracks in the walls to missing tiles. Generally, you have one year to amend your claim if you find additional damage. It can be helpful, if tedious, to prepare for this possibility ahead of time by videotaping the contents and condition of your home and keeping records on the details of your major purchases. A safe-deposit box is a good place to keep these items.

You said jewelry might be restricted, and I found out that in fact it is restricted in my policy. My insurance company will only pay up to $1,000 for all jewelry, and I know my engagement ring alone is worth more than that. How can I increase this protection?
All policies limit the amount of money your insurance company would pay for specific items, such as jewelry or computer equipment. If the standard coverage is too low for your comfort, you can buy additional protection by adding an amendment called an endorsement to protect a particular item (for example, your engagement ring). But please make sure that it's really worth paying the extra premiums to extend your coverage on the items.

What is off-premise protection?

This facet of your homeowner's policy covers your possessions outside your house. For example, if you are mugged on the street or your luggage is stolen on vacation, off-premise protection should reimburse you for the items you lose. If you need to pay extra for this coverage, think carefully about the size of the deductible and the likelihood that you would be carrying around items that are worth more. If the deductible is pretty high, and you don't normally run around wearing or carrying a lot of expensive stuff, it might not be worth it. And be careful if the big-ticket items you do tend to travel with include your engagement ring or your laptop computer. If they are only covered up to a certain level and you haven't extended their protection, a high deductible on top of the reimbursement restriction could make this coverage a waste of time.

What is additional living expense protection?

In the event your home is damaged, your insurer will reimburse you for the costs associated with maintaining a temporary residence elsewhere while repairs are made on your home. Some policies offer unlimited coverage, whereby you are reimbursed for the total cost of necessary expenses, without a time limitation. The most common loss of use coverage seen on homeowner's policies is coverage for a dollar amount equal to 20 percent or 30 percent of the dwelling limit listed on the policy.

When I purchased my home, my bank required me to get a certain level of homeowner's insurance, so that's what I got. If it weren't enough, wouldn't they have made me purchase more?

If your coverage isn't enough to cover the bank's potential loss, yes, they probably would require you to buy more coverage.

But don't rely on the bank to tell you what amount of insurance you need. The bank only cares about covering the loan amount. You have additional needs: protecting your personal property, having solid additional expense coverage, and making sure your policy keeps up with rising building costs.

Bottom line, financially, what should I look for in homeowner's insurance?
You want to be able to replace your home and its contents if something should happen to your house. The cost of doing that after a catastrophic loss will probably be greater than the depreciated cash value of your property. This means that, as usual, you want replacement-cost coverage. You also want to have automatic inflation adjustments built into your policy.

Umbrella Policies

Umbrella insurance acts as a shield for your assets if you are sued. It is an extra layer of liability protection that kicks in when your other insurance policies, such as homeowner's or auto, have reached their limits.

What does an umbrella policy cover?
An umbrella policy can offer coverage into the millions of dollars in case you are sued under either your homeowner's or auto insurance policy as the result of an accident or injury—including one involving a natural disaster, such as a storm that blows a tree, for example, onto a neighbor's house. The amount of coverage offered by umbrella policies varies, and the types of accidents a policy covers also vary.

I thought I was covered by my homeowner's or auto policy for liability. Why do I need an umbrella policy?
Most homeowner's and auto insurance policies do offer some liability protection, but the coverage may not be enough to protect your assets in case of a suit. An umbrella policy provides protection that is over and above that of your normal auto and home insurance coverage, and that kicks in after your homeowner's or auto insurance policy has paid its maximum amount.

Let's say, for example, that you are a homeowner and your homeowner's policy insures you for liability up to a maximum amount of $500,000. If a person injures herself on your property, sues you for $1 million, and wins the lawsuit, without an umbrella policy it might be up to you to come up with the additional $500,000. If you have assets—such as a vacation home, investments, or a 401(k)—you could risk losing them to pay the uncovered portion of the judgment. If you own enough umbrella insurance, however, you will be covered for the difference. That's why, if you're considering an umbrella policy, I recommend buying a policy that fully protects you. Your combined insurance policies—homeowner's, auto, and umbrella insurance—should cover a maximum amount equal to at least the amount of your net worth.

How much will an umbrella policy pay?
Umbrella coverage ranges from $1 million to $5 million or more. And there may be additional costs; most insurance companies require you to have a certain amount of regular insurance coverage before you purchase an umbrella policy, so you may need to upgrade to the maximum coverage for both your home and your car, which can be costly.

How much does it cost?
You can expect to pay between about $150 and $300 a year for $1 million in coverage, about $225 to $375 a year for $2 mil-

lion in coverage, and about $50 more a year for every additional $1 million in coverage after that.

Do umbrella policies carry high deductibles?
There isn't a deductible per se. The idea that your liability coverage on your home and auto policies is used first to settle a judgment. Only after you have used up the coverage from those policies does your umbrella coverage kick in. Essentially, the amount of liability coverage stated on your primary auto and home policies is the umbrella deductible.

How do I decide whether I need umbrella insurance?
One issue to consider is whether you're susceptible to being sued for a large amount of money. Do you have a significant estate or substantial future earning power? If so, you might want to consider protecting it. Certain activities also put you at increased risk for a suit. Do you have clients, employees, or even friends with young children who visit your home often? Do you have neighbors, and would any damage to their homes be expensive to repair? Do you drive a car every day? Do you have a child who will soon be driving?

If you answer yes to one or all of these questions, you may want to think seriously about an umbrella policy. Given the potential catastrophes an extra policy can help you to avoid, the added expense may be well worth the cost. If you answered no to all of the questions, it may be wisest to stick with the coverage you already have.

How much umbrella liability coverage should I buy?
Remember that you're covering damages to others. Do you live in a wealthy town, where you could be an easy target for a big settlement? Do you travel a lot? Do you entertain a lot? Do you operate a home-based business and have employees or

clients coming to your home on a regular basis? (Many self-employed people wrongly assume that this is covered in their homeowner's policy.) If you answered yes to any of these questions, it is particularly important for you to have umbrella liability insurance.

But how much to buy is a decision that you should make with a financial professional, for there is no set formula.

MORTGAGE PROTECTION INSURANCE

What is the difference between private mortgage insurance and mortgage protection insurance?

If you bought your home without putting down at least 20 percent of its cost, you probably had to buy private mortgage insurance (PMI) to get your mortgage and you probably had to pay it until you had at least 20 percent equity in your home (and you had to initiate the cancellation process). Such insurance protects the lender in case you stop making your mortgage payments and the house goes into foreclosure. Some insurance agencies will offer to sell you after-death mortgage protection insurance, which is basically an arrangement where you pay your premiums and, should you die before your mortgage is paid and while your policy is still in effect, the insurance company pays off whatever is left on your mortgage.

Do the premiums on mortgage protection insurance go down as the balance on my mortgage goes down?

No. Your premiums will stay the same, because they are calculated with that decrease in mind.

How do I know if I need after-death mortgage protection insurance?

Most likely you do not, although you need to consider your individual situation. Do you have beneficiaries who will need a place to live without worrying about making mortgage payments? Still, in that case, I think it makes more sense to buy a good term life insurance policy that includes enough money to pay off your mortgage as well as provide for your family's other needs after you are gone.

We just refinanced our mortgage. What happens to our old mortgage protection insurance?

If you still want to keep it, call your insurance company. You will probably be able to get a new policy with a lower premium.

Is there any way to reduce my premiums on mortgage protection insurance?

Some companies do offer a modest reduction if you and your spouse both have this type of coverage. But if you have made the decision to protect your home this way instead of just covering this cost on your term life insurance policy, consider whether you both really need it. If you both contribute equally to paying your mortgage, then maybe it makes sense, but if you do not work outside the home, for example, it doesn't make sense for both of you have this coverage because, presumably, your working spouse will be able to continue working and making these payments after you are gone.

You keep mentioning that increasing my deductible will reduce my premium costs. Can you be more specific about what that means in terms of homeowner's insurance?

If you raise your deductible from $250 to $500 you can reduce your premiums by about 10 percent. Raise the deductible to $1,000 and you may be able to reduce your premium by 20 percent. A $2,500 deductible could cut your premium by 30 percent. Remember, you are taking a gamble that you will save more on your premiums than you will ultimately wind up paying in deductibles. Just be sure that you will actually be able to pay the deductible if you need to.

How can I save on homeowner's insurance?

If you can afford it, raise your deductible. You may be able to get a discount if you buy your homeowner's and car insurance from the same company—but make sure both policies compare favorably to others you're considering. Take steps to make your home safe: Buy fire extinguishers, and install smoke detectors, security systems, and deadbolt locks. And this is yet another good reason not to smoke. Ask your insurance agent about these measures; you may find that they all translate into cost reductions. Ask about senior citizen reductions and loyal customer reductions if you have been with your insurance company for at least five years, and investigate whether any associations you belong to offer discounted group coverage. Finally, here's a common mistake: Don't include the value of your land when you are figuring out how much insurance to purchase. Your lot isn't included in the coverage, so it doesn't make sense to pay as though it were.

Renter's Insurance

I don't own a home—I rent. Do I need renter's insurance?

If you had personal property that was damaged by a fire or you were robbed, how much would it cost you to replace what you own? It doesn't matter whether the home your possessions are in belongs to you or someone else, right? Many renter's insurance policies also contain some liability protection for you as well, in case you damage your apartment or in case someone else is hurt in your apartment. If you have anything of value that you want to protect then, in my opinion, renter's insurance is a good thing.

Does renter's insurance just cover my personal property?

Actually, no. Usually there is liability and medical payments coverage, in case someone injures himself in your apartment and sues you along with the landlord. Also, renter's insurance can cover your loss of use if something catastrophic should happen to the building and you were forced to live somewhere else while the owners repair or rebuild it. This can be key protection for renters, since you often don't have as much control over the maintenance of your property and its systems as owners do.

FLOOD INSURANCE

I am about to buy a home in what they call a low- to medium-risk area for floods. Do I need flood insurance?

I think you do. Between 20 and 25 percent of the flood insurance claims come from low- to medium-risk areas.

If I do not have flood insurance, is there a national program that will help me in case of a natural disaster?

Yes, if your area is declared a federal disaster area, then you can get help through the Federal Emergency Management

Agency (FEMA), *www.fema.gov*, from the crippling financial losses often caused by flooding.

If FEMA will give me money to replace my home, why should I pay for private flood insurance?

Because floods are often too small or too localized to qualify for federal assistance. More to the point, even if a flood does qualify, the assistance from FEMA comes in the form of a loan or small grant. In fact, grants are usually given in amounts that barely cover losses, much less enable you to rebuild. And disaster home loans, with an average repayment plan of 18.5 years, must be repaid with interest on top of your existing mortgage payment.

The bottom line is that there is a big difference between paying back a loan, even if it is at a low interest rate, and having an insurance plan that will pay for everything.

How much does a flood insurance policy cost?

The average flood insurance premium costs about $500 a year for an average of $100,000 of coverage. Contrast that with the cost of taking out a FEMA loan of just $50,000 to help you replace your articles lost in a flood. Such a loan would cost you an average of $240 a month for an average repayment period of close to 30 years!

Does FEMA offer flood insurance?

Yes. Under FEMA's National Flood Insurance Program (NFIP), federally backed flood insurance is available in communities that adopt and enforce regulations to reduce flood losses. The good news is that more than 20,000 communities in the United States and its territories that are faced with potential flooding participate in the NFIP, so the chances are excellent that NFIP insurance is available to you.

For more information about NFIP flood insurance and to find out if it is available in your particular area, call the NFIP at (888) 379-9531. Believe it or not, you will get a live person on the phone (as of the writing of this book) who can answer your questions.

I am about to buy a home in a high-risk flood area and my mortgage broker is telling me that I have to buy flood insurance. Is this correct?
Yes, if you are buying a house in a designated high-risk area and receive a mortgage loan from a federally regulated lender, your lender must, by law, require that you buy flood insurance.

What is the maximum flood insurance I can buy?

- Up to $250,000 for single-family, two-to-four family, and other residential buildings
- Up to $500,000 for nonresidential buildings, including small businesses
- Up to $100,000 for contents coverage for residences for owners and/or renters
- Up to $500,000 for contents for businesses, including small businesses

If I am a renter in a high-risk flood area, can I buy flood insurance?
Yes.

If I hear on the news that a flooding is expected in my area, can I get a policy right away?
No. Policies go into effect 30 days after the policy is purchased. So please do not wait until you are faced with an emergency to get yourself covered.

If I own my home outright and I live in a high-risk flood area, am I still required to buy flood insurance?
If you own your house outright, no federal agency will force you to buy flood insurance or keep the flood insurance you had to have when you still had a mortgage. Property owners who do not have a mortgage insured by a federal agency are free to buy the insurance or not buy the insurance—it all depends on your assessment of the risk that you will be taking.

Earthquake Insurance

Many of us trust that after a natural disaster, the government will step in with aid so that any financial losses we suffer will eventually be recouped. That is not generally true. The government is likely to provide disaster assistance, but it does not protect the individual homeowner from loss. The most common federal aid after a disaster comes in the form of low-interest loans, which must be paid back over time.

In the last decade, the insurance industry has paid out record amounts of money for insured losses caused by earthquakes and hurricanes. With respect to earthquakes, the industry has come up with two main ways to deal with the possibilities of large losses. Some insurers simply won't accept new policies or renewals in areas of high seismic risk. Others have been working with Congress to establish a federal natural disaster insurance program to augment the capacity of private industry to provide disaster insurance. If you live in an area that is prone to earthquakes, you should be aware of the following information about earthquake insurance. Please note: While the principles of earthquake insurance are the same in every state, the specifics about coverage, availability, and affordability vary from company to company and state to state.

Who sells earthquake insurance?

In general, only large multi-line, multi-state companies insure catastrophes. And among these, fewer still sell earthquake insurance. Even in California, which is the most earthquake-prone of all our states, only about 175 insurers actively sell earthquake insurance, out of a total of about 800 property/casualty insurers and about 700 life and health insurers.

In the future, Congress may pass legislation creating a federally backed insurance program but, as of the writing of this book, that has not yet happened, though a new state-managed program has just been initiated in California.

I have been offered earthquake insurance from a small insurance company and the rates are far better than those I've been offered by a large company. Which way should I go?

Watch out. Small insurance companies usually lack the financial resources to pay for a large catastrophic event. It's better to stay away from small insurers offering earthquake coverage.

What does a typical earthquake insurance policy cover?

A typical earthquake policy insures for loss against structural damage, damage to contents, and loss of use (residential) or business income (commercial).

What does loss of use or business income coverage mean?

Loss of use covers the costs of a hotel or other rental and meals until the structure is repaired. Business income covers the income and rental losses arising from the shutdown of the business (sometimes called business interruption).

Everyone tells me that earthquake insurance is not worth it because of the high deductible. Do you agree?
It is true that earthquake insurance policies have high deductibles. A typical deductible is 10 to 15 percent of the value of your property. So if your home is worth $200,000 and your deductible is 10 percent, then you would be responsible for the first 10 percent (or $20,000) worth of damage to that home before your policy would kick in. The same would be true for the contents of your home. The reason that many people say it is not worth it is that for a well-built wood-frame house, this deductible generally exceeds the structural loss for most moderate earthquakes. Due to improvements in structural soundness and design, recent earthquakes have caused less damage to structures than to the contents within those structures.

I live in California and was just offered a policy by the CEA. What is the CEA?
Pressure put on state officials by insurance carriers to carry earthquake insurance has resulted in the creation of the California Earthquake Authority (CEA). This new agency provides "mini" earthquake insurance policies, not covering pools, patios, fences, driveways, or detached garages. These policies have a 15 percent deductible, cover no more than $5,000 worth of a home's contents, and provide a maximum of $1,500 in living expenses.

The rating plan approved by CEA has a statewide average rate of $2.79 for every $1,000 of coverage, with homeowners in low-risk areas paying less and those in high-risk areas paying more. If an earthquake produces more claims than available resources can handle and you have a CEA policy, you may be required to pay an assessment, which could add up to as much as 20 percent to future earthquake premiums. The cost of these new policies varies throughout the state, depending on the earthquake risk and the age and construction of the home.

What questions should I ask an agent when buying an earthquake policy?

- Why should I buy earthquake insurance?
- Is there another way for me to replace my property if I don't have earthquake insurance?
- Is the earthquake insurance coverage included in my existing homeowner's policy or do I have to buy a separate policy?
- What will earthquake insurance cover?
- How much earthquake insurance coverage should I buy?
- How much will it cost me annually?
- Will the coverage I buy apply to the combined value of my house (the structure itself) and the contents of my home (furniture, clothing, electronic equipment, collections, etc.), or should I evaluate my potential losses separately?
- How much is the deductible?
- Is the deductible for my earthquake insurance coverage different from the deductible for my basic homeowner's coverage?
- How is the deductible on my earthquake insurance coverage going to be calculated in the event of a loss? Will a separate deductible apply to the structure, contents, and detached structures, or does one deductible apply to the entire loss?

- Does the policy have a guaranteed replacement cost coverage? If so, how would this coverage apply if I suffered a loss?
- If you own a condominium, ask how earthquake insurance would benefit you. (Ask specifically what insurance would cover if you were forced to vacate the premises for safety reasons.)
- If you're a renter, ask how earthquake insurance would benefit you. (Ask specifically if additional living expenses would be covered if you were forced to vacate the premises for safety reasons.)
- Will my car be covered by earthquake insurance?
- What about other structures the garage, for instance? Would it be covered by the same policy or will I need to get a separate policy or add a rider to my primary policy?
- If I have to vacate my home, will earthquake insurance cover the hotel expenses? If so, for how long?
- Is breakage of fragile articles covered if I purchase earthquake insurance? Is there a better way to cover these items?
- Does the type of home I live in (brick, veneer, masonry) or whether my home is bolted to the foundation affect the premiums or benefits of earthquake coverage?
- Does the earthquake policy exclude certain repairs?
- How long do I have to wait after an earthquake before I can file a claim?
- What about aftershocks that can be attributed to the original quake? Would I be covered for resulting damages without another deductible?
- Are there additional "endorsements" to the earthquake coverage that I should also consider, such as building code upgrades, structural report coverage, demolition, etc.?

Miscellaneous Private Insurance

My company has just developed something called a "cafeteria plan" that gives employees the option to choose our benefits now, including some insurance options. How will this work?

Each plan is different, but generally, these plans offer a menu of flexible benefit options for employees. You may be able to choose within a particular type of insurance, such as a standard health insurance plan, an HMO, and a PPO, or you may be able to choose among different types of insurance benefits, like life or disability. You generally get a specific number of points or credits that you can use to customize your benefits. You'll need to consider the needs of your family carefully when choosing the form your benefits will take, but you're lucky to have the flexibility. Make the most of it.

My company offers flexible spending accounts, but they seem like a lot of trouble. Are they worth it?

Flexible spending accounts are funds in which you can have your employer deduct money from your paycheck on a before-tax basis for you to use to pay for your out-of-pocket medical expenses, your copayments, or other related health-care expenses such as eyeglasses, or for child-care or other dependent-care expenses. This is your money and you can choose how much to withhold from your paycheck. The savings come because you aren't paying taxes on this money, which can save you hundreds of dollars over the course of the year. The catch is that you must submit paperwork to be reimbursed and you must use all the money you set aside in 12 to 15 months; otherwise you lose it, so be careful in estimating your expenses. If your company offers this benefit, try it out the first year with a relatively small contribution to your fund and see how it feels. You may find that the bit of extra trouble is worth the savings and, as a bonus, it may help you realistically identify how much your medical or dependent-care expenses actually cost you each year, since you're keeping track.

When my daughter got engaged, a friend told us about wedding insurance. It sounds silly, but we are spending an awful lot of money on this celebration. Should I investigate further?

This is something to consider. The principal idea of wedding insurance is that it will protect you if a wedding guest is injured and sues you or will reimburse your unrefundable deposits if you have to cancel the plans (though not if the bride and/or groom change their minds and decide not to marry). Some homeowner's insurance policies will cover the liability of the reception, should a guest injure himself, but filing a liability claim will likely result in either a significantly higher renewal premium or the actual cancellation of the homeowner's policy. Wedding insurance policies typically range anywhere from $185 to about $500.

My daughter is going to be a college freshman in the fall. We got some information in the mail about tuition insurance. What do you think about it?

Not much. Tuition insurance would reimburse you for the money you've spent on tuition (and usually room, board, and fees) if your daughter were to drop out of school before a given semester ends due to illness or injury, in exchange for a premium of about 1 percent of the semester's costs. It's your decision, but I think this insurance is basically unnecessary. Keep in mind that a semester is only three or four months long and that most universities will refund tuition, at least partially, if a student withdraws within the first four to six weeks. Also, if your daughter becomes sick or injured during the last few weeks of a semester, it is often possible to arrange for her to complete her course work and exams during the following semester at no extra cost (just extra work for her!). If you compare this policy to, say, term life insurance, you'll see that you would be paying a relatively high premium for pretty modest coverage over a short period of time.

You probably think that cancer insurance is a bad investment too. But there is a history of cancer in my family, and I have seen how some of my relatives suffered financially after an illness. This might not be for everyone, but shouldn't I consider this protection?

Of course the last thing you want to worry about when you are really sick is money. But that is why you have comprehensive health coverage! Cancer insurance preys on your fear of cancer, but if you have good general health insurance you should already be protected in case you develop cancer or any other debilitating illness. Why should you pay twice for the same coverage? And if you don't have coverage, why buy narrow protection from only one disease when you can buy expansive protection?

What is a rated policy?

This is a type of policy that may be offered to you if you have some type of unusual risk factor, like a dangerous job or poor health, and usually comes with relatively high premiums.

My travel agent always encourages me to buy flight insurance. Do I really need it?

No way. Flight insurance exploits your fear of flying. As you have probably heard before, your chances of dying in a car are much greater than your chances of being in a plane crash. In any case, a good term life insurance policy will cover you in the air and on the ground. Check to see if your life insurance policy has an aviation clause. The credit card you use to pay for your airline ticket may also provide this type of coverage for no fee, so check your membership agreement.

When I rent cars, I'm never sure if I should pay for the rental car liability or collision insurance. What do you think?

I think you absolutely need liability coverage on a rental car, but you often don't need to buy it from the rental company. Many comprehensive auto liability policies cover you when you rent a car. Check to make sure that yours does and then don't duplicate this coverage at the rental counter. Your car insurance may also cover comprehensive collision in a rental car, so check that out too.

Does my credit card cover the insurance that I need for a rental car?

Your credit card may provide such coverage as long as you use it to pay for the car rental. If you pay for a rental car with an American Express green card, for example, and you are not a student, you will be covered for collision and damage but not liability. Do some research with your credit card company; the chances are that you've got this covered.

ADDITIONAL RESOURCES

Health Insurance Association of America
1201 F Street NW, Suite 500
Washington, DC 20004-1204
(202) 824-1600
www.hiaa.org

National Council on Aging
300 D Street NW, Suite 801
Washington, DC 20024
(202) 479-1200
www.ncoa.org

National Association of Insurance Commissioners
444 N. Capitol Street, Suite 701
Washington, DC 20001-1512
(202) 624-7790
www.naic.org

The State Health Insurance Advisory Program (SHIP)
This is a government program that provides information on Medicare to the elderly and disabled. Each state has its own hot-

line. You can call (800) 677-1116 to find out which organization you should call in your state for this service.

The National Committee for Quality Assurance
(HMOs and other MCOs)
2000 L Street NW, Suite 500
Washington, DC 20036
(888) 275-7585
www.ncqa.org

Community Health Accreditation Program
(home health care and nursing homes)
1300 19th Street NW, Suite 150
Washington, DC 20036
(800) 656-9656
www.chapinc.org

For information on Medicare in English and Spanish from the Health Care Financing Administration: (800) 633-4227. People who require TDD or TTY can call (877) 486-2048.

Assisted Living

American Association of Homes and Services for the Aging
2519 Connecticut Avenue NW
Washington, DC 20008
(202) 783-2242
www.aahsa.org
Publishes pamphlets on senior care options.

American Bar Association Commission on Law and Aging
740 15th Street NW
Washington, DC 20005-1022
(202) 662-8690
www.abanet.org/aging
Offers pamphlets on legal rights and care of elders.

Assisted Living Federation of America
1650 King Street, Suite 602
Alexandria, VA 22314-2747
(703) 894-1805
www.alfa.org
Offers pamphlets and a listing of member facilities by state; also publishes the industry magazine, *Assisted Living Today.*

National Academy of Elder Law Attorneys, Inc.
1604 North Country Club Road
Tuscon, Arizona 85716
(520) 881-4005
www.naela.org
To find an attorney who can review an assisted-living contract. This organization also offers a brochure: *Questions and Answers When Looking for an Elder Law Attorney.*

WEBSITES

www.healthinsuranceinfo.net
Maintained by Georgetown University, this site includes state-specific insurance information.

www.healthinsurance.org
The Questions section provides clear explanations of key insurance terms and topics.

www.aarp.org
This site has up-to-date information on Medicare policy changes, as well as articles and resources on all insurance issues at *www.aarp.org/healthcoverage/.*

www.ehealthinsurance.com
Shop online for a health insurance policy.

www.insure.com
This site has a database of articles about insurance.

Insurance Rating Services

A.M. Best
(908) 439-2200
www.ambest.com

Moody's
(212) 553-0300
www.moodys.com

Standard & Poor's
(212) 438-2400
www.standardandpoors.com

Companies That Sell Long-term Care Insurance

Genworth Financial
(888) 436-9678
(800) GENWORTH
www.genworth.com

John Hancock
www.johnhancocklongtermcare.com

Metropolitan Life
(800) 638-5433
www.metlife.com

www.longtermcarewiz.com
Contains educational information, as well as policy quote service.

www.longtermcareinsurance.org
A not-for-profit organization with a search engine to help consumers shop for policies.

Books

Consumer Reports Complete Guide to Health Services for Seniors, edited by Trudy Lieberman. This guide details what your family needs to know about Medicare, assisted living, nursing homes, home care, and adult day care.

Insurance companies, agents, and policies are primarily regulated by state, not federal, laws. Each state has a department of insurance that is responsible for such regulation. Be sure to consult the department in your state and an expert in the laws of your state when you are making decisions about your own insurance needs.

State Insurance Departments
(800 numbers are only valid in-state)

Alabama
(334) 269-3550
www.aldoi.gov

Alaska
(907) 465-2515
www.dced.state.ak.us/insurance

Arizona
(800) 325-2548
www.id.state.az.us

Arkansas
(501) 371-2600 or (800) 282-9134
www.arkansas.gov/insurance

California
(800) 927-4357
www.insurance.ca.gov

Colorado
(800) 930-3745
www.dora.state.co.us/insurance

Delaware
(302) 739-4251
www.state.de.us/inscom/index.html

District of Columbia
(202) 727-8002
www.disr.washingtondc.gov

Florida
(800) 342-2762
www.floir.com/

Georgia
(404) 656-2056 or (800) 656-2298
www.inscomm.state.ga.us

Hawaii
(808) 586-2790
www.state.hi.us/dcca/ins

Idaho
(208) 334-2250
www.doi.state.id.us

Illinois
(866) 445-5364
www.ins.state.il.us

Indiana
(317) 232-2385
www.ai.org/idoi/

Iowa
(515) 281-5705 or (877) 955-1212
www.iid.state.ia.us

Kansas
(785) 296-3071 or (800) 432-2484
www.ksinsurance.org

Kentucky
(800) 595-6053
doi.ppr.ky.gov/kentucky

Louisiana
(225) 342-0895 or (800) 259-5301
www.ldi.state.la.us

Maine
(207) 582-8707
www.state.me.us/pfr/ins/ins_index.htm

Maryland
(410) 333-6200 or (800) 492-6116
www.mdinsurance.state.md.us

Massachusetts
(617) 973-8787 or (888) 283-3757
www.state.ma.us/consumer/Info/insur.htm

Michigan
(517) 335-4978 or (877) 999-6442
www.michigan.gov/cis

Minnesota
(651) 296-2488
www.state.mn.us

Mississippi
(601) 359-3569 or (800) 562-2957
www.doi.state.ms.us

Missouri
(800) 726-7390
www.insurance.state.mo.us

Montana
(800) 332-6148
www.state.mt.us

Nebraska
(402) 471-2201
www.nol.org/home/NDOI/

Nevada
(775) 687-4270 or (800) 992-0900
doi.state.nv.us

New Hampshire
(603) 271-2261 or (800) 852-3416
www.state.nh.us/insurance/

New Jersey
(609) 292-5360
www.state.nj.us/dobi/index.shtml

New Mexico
(505) 827-4601 or (800) 947-4722
www.nmprc.state.nm.us/insurance/inshm.htm

New York
(800) 342-3736
www.ins.state.ny.us

North Carolina
(919) 733-2032 or (800) 546-5664
www.ncdoi.com

North Dakota
(800) 247-0560
www.state.nd.us/ndins

Ohio
(614) 644-2658 or (800) 686-1526
www.ohioinsurance.gov

Oklahoma
(800) 522-0071 or (405) 521-2828
www.oid.state.ok.us

Oregon
(503) 947-7980
www.cbs.state.or.us/external/ins/index.html

Pennsylvania
(877) 881-6388
www.ins.state.pa.us/ins

Rhode Island
(401) 222-5475
www.dbr.state.ri.us

South Carolina
(803) 737-6160
www.doi.state.sc.us

South Dakota
(605) 773-5369
www.state.sd.us/drr2/reg/insurance/

Tennessee
(615) 741-6007
www.state.tn.us/commerce/insurance/

Texas
(512) 463-6169 or (800) 252-3439
www.tdi.state.tx.us/

Utah
(801) 538-3800
www.insurance.utah.gov

Vermont
(802) 828-3301
www.bishca.state.vt.us

Virginia
(800) 552-7945
www.state.va.us/scc/division/boi/

Washington
(800) 562-6900
www.insurance.wa.gov

West Virginia
(800) 642-9004 or (304) 558-3354
www.wvinsurance.gov

Wisconsin
(800) 236-8517
oci.wi.gov/oci_home.htm

Wyoming
(307) 777-7401 or (800) 438-5768
insurance.state.wy.us

INDEX

About Suze Orman

Suze Orman has been called "a force in the world of personal finance" and a "one-woman financial advice powerhouse" by *USA Today*. A two-time Emmy® Award–winning television show host, *New York Times* best-selling author, magazine and online columnist, writer-producer, and motivational speaker, Suze is undeniably America's most recognized personal finance expert.

Suze has written five consecutive *New York Times* best sellers—*The Money Book for the Young, Fabulous & Broke*; *The Laws of Money, The Lessons of Life*; *The Road to Wealth*; *The Courage to Be Rich*; and *The 9 Steps to Financial Freedom*—as well as the national best sellers *Suze Orman's Financial Guidebook* and *You've Earned It, Don't Lose It.* Her most recent book, *Women & Money*, was published by Spiegel & Grau in February 2007. A newspaper column, also called "Women & Money," syndicated by Universal Press Syndicate, began in January 2007. Additionally, she has created *Suze Orman's*

FICO Kit, Suze Orman's Will & Trust Kit, Suze Orman's Insurance Kit, The Ask Suze Library System, and *Suze Orman's Ultimate Protection Portfolio.*

Suze has written, coproduced, and hosted five PBS specials based on her *New York Times* best-selling books. She is the single most successful fund-raiser in the history of public television, and recently won her second Daytime Emmy® Award in the category of Outstanding Service Show Host. Suze won her first Emmy® in 2004, in the same category.

Suze is a contributing editor to *O, The Oprah Magazine* and *O at Home* and has a biweekly column, "Money Matters," on Yahoo! Finance. Suze hosts her own award-winning national CNBC-TV show, *The Suze Orman Show*, which airs every Saturday night, as well as *Financial Freedom Hour* on QVC television.

Suze has been honored with three American Women in Radio and Television (AWRT) Gracie Allen Awards. This award recognizes the nation's best radio, television, and cable programming for, by, and about women. In 2003, Suze garnered her first Gracie for *The Suze Orman Show* in the National/Network/Sydication Talk show category. She won her second and third Gracies in the Individual Achievement: Program Host category in 2005 and 2006.

Profiled in *Worth* magazine's 100th issue as among those "who have revolutionized the way America thinks about money," Suze also was named one of *Smart Money* magazine's top thirty "Power Brokers," defined as those who have most influenced the mutual fund industry and affected our money, in 1999. A 2003 inductee into the Books for a Better Life (BBL) Award Hall of Fame in recognition of her ongoing contributions to self-improvement, Suze previously received the 1999 BBL Motivational Book Award for *The Courage to Be Rich.* As a tribute to her continuing involvement, in 2002 the organization established the Suze Orman First Book Award to honor a first-time author of a self-improvement book in any category. She received a 2003 Crossing Borders Award from the Feminist Press. The award recognizes a distinguished group of women who not only have excelled in remarkable careers but also have shown great courage, vision, and conviction by forging new places for women in their respective fields. In 2002, Suze was selected as one of five distinguished recipients of the prestigious TJFR Group News Luminaries Award, which honors lifetime achievement in business journalism.

A sought-after motivational speaker, Suze has lectured widely throughout the United States, South Africa, and Asia to audiences of up to fifty thousand people, often appearing alongside individuals such as Colin Powell, Rudy Giuliani, Jerry Lewis, Steve Forbes, and Donald Trump. She has been featured in almost every major publication in the United States and has appeared numerous times on *The View*, *Larry King Live*, and *The Oprah Winfrey Show*.

A Certified Financial Planner®, Suze directed the Suze Orman Financial Group from 1987 to 1997, served as vice president of investments for Prudential Bache Securities from 1983 to 1987, and from 1980 to 1983 was an account executive at Merrill Lynch. Prior to that, she worked as a waitress at the Buttercup Bakery in Berkeley, California, from 1973 to 1980.